Preface ·

For as long as I can remember, I have been intrigued by the question of God's existence and by the equally compelling question of what God might be like, should God exist. I have discovered that I am not alone in this fascination.

Many fellow-enquirers are strongly repelled by any suggestion that they must first follow the teachings of a particular religion in order to discover what God might be like. I agree with them, while at the same time acknowledging that for almost all my life, I have been, in some form or other, a Christian.

This book has been born out of numerous conversations with honest enquirers, fearful doubters, ardent believers and convinced atheists. More than that, it has been born out of a desire to conduct a personal, open and honest enquiry into the possible existence and nature of God. This is not a work of Christian apologetics; I am not attempting to convince anyone of anything. Rather, it is an invitation to look over my shoulder as I think my way through what I consider to be the most important issues with regard to belief in God.

As I wrote (and rewrote) this book, I made every effort to identify prior convictions and prejudices and then to set them to one side. What emerged was, for me, a fascinating process that led me down new roads and, I believe into green, if somewhat uncomfortable pastures. I hope that it encourages others to make a similar journey.

Brendan McCarthy

THE
GOD
ENQUIRY

Brendan McC...

THE
GOD
ENQUIRY

BRENDAN McCARTHY

Matador
9 Priory Business Park
Kibworth Beauchamp
Leicestershire LE8 0RX, UK
Tel: (+44) 116 279 2299
Fax: (+44) 116 279 2277
Email: books@troubador.co.uk
Web: www.troubador.co.uk/matador

ISBN 978 1783062 768

British Library Cataloguing in Publication Data.
A catalogue record for this book is available from the British Library.

Typeset in Aldine401 BT Roman by Troubador Publishing Ltd
Printed and bound in the UK by TJ International, Padstow, Cornwall

Matador is an imprint of Troubador Publishing Ltd

Contents

Part One

Is there Room in the Universe for God?

Chapter One

Getting Started – The Nature of the Enquiry

(Personal Engagement with Questions of Belief…Reason, Intuition and Experience… Why Choose to Explore Christian Theology?)

A Shock to the System

As I begin to write this book I am, by temperament and inclination an atheist; by persuasion I am a *Christian*. It took me some time to realise that this is who and what I am and even longer to become comfortable with it.

I can remember vividly when I first became aware of this internal tension. I was nineteen and on my way home to Ireland from Israel, hitch-hiking across Europe as students in the nineteen seventies were wont to do. I had spent almost a month bivouacking in 'the Holy Land' seeing the sights, meeting Jews, Christians and Muslims as I and four friends begged lifts around Israel/Palestine just three years after the Yom Kippur war of 1973. As there were five of us, we had to take it in turns to hitch-hike solo. It was just after I had completed one such solo leg of the journey home, somewhere west of Athens that the thought quite suddenly came to me: *'It's all a load of nonsense'*.

Up until then I had been more than happy to accept a traditional form of Christianity with its attendant perspectives on life as being, literally, the gospel truth; indeed, on numerous occasions, defending it vigorously, against what I considered to be unwarranted atheistic attacks. Being immersed in the Bible lands had, I thought, strengthened that viewpoint, but, clearly, as I emerged from adolescence into adulthood (things took a little longer back then), something was stirring in my mind. I had just completed the first year of a theology degree at the Queen's University of Belfast and this had included an Introduction to Philosophy course. I wasn't consciously aware of any great impact that this had made on my thinking, and my grade at the end of the year did nothing to dispel this notion, but it seems that at some deeper level I was genuinely wrestling with questions of belief and faith: questions of reality.

The immediate impact on me was, to say the least, disturbing. Truth to be told, given the previous certainty with which I had held beliefs that had been with me since my childhood, I was more than a little panic-stricken. Unwelcome thoughts and their even more unwelcome implications kept tumbling through my head, refusing to go away: *there was no God, whatever else Jesus was, he wasn't the Son of God or Saviour of the world, there was no life after death and, my life, the lives of my friends and family, indeed the whole of human history was without any ultimate meaning or significance.* I vividly remember the middle-of-the-night panics that ensued for a few days as I grappled with the entire centre of my universe not only shifting, but having been removed, erased and excised from the new reality that I was struggling to come to terms with. I had previously harboured vague thoughts of being ordained; I certainly had not contemplated abandoning my theology degree. Now the first of these seemed to be entirely out of the question and I was not enamoured with the prospect of studying to degree level a subject that was, essentially, based on an illusion. Needless to say, the whole thing had a dampening effect on the remainder of my vacation and I eventually returned to Ireland after six weeks of outdoor living; fit and healthy and with something resembling a tan, but with a bit of my customary zest for life subdued.

As if recovering from the first impact of an earthquake, still wary of any aftershocks, I simply survived the first few weeks following the discovery of my startling new conviction. Then, slowly realising that the world had not stopped turning, that I was still able to enjoy breathing and being alive, being with my friends and getting on with the normal business of life, I peeked out through my fingers and dared to look at the shocking thought that had turned my world on its head. Where had it come from? Why had it lodged itself in my mind with such strength? Was it always lurking there, ready to ambush me once I dropped my guard? Why did I now think it was true? How might I begin to know whether or not it *was* true?

Thereafter, began a process that has, ever since, been a constant feature of my life: a continual examination and re-examination of Christian faith and theology, putting under scrutiny not only its credibility but also its interpretation and practice. Like the proverbial painting of the Forth or Golden Gate bridges this has been a never-ending process; once I finish one round of investigation, I catch my breath for a little while and then start again. As I write this introductory chapter, I remain, by inclination an atheist, but by conviction a *Christian*. What I shall be by the time I have completed this book, I *genuinely* do not know. This might seem to be a hollow statement, but I can honestly say that it is true. In writing this book, I am inviting others to follow me in a journey of exploration. I shall not be trying to *defend* a Christian understanding of God; I shall be *investigating* it.

Such constant cycles of exploring and re-exploring the same thing might give the impression that I am a completely neurotic individual given to sitting in dark corners muttering incomprehensively to myself while obsessively going over the same theories, arguments and explanations. Not so. I am a relatively 'normal' person with a wife and family; the closest I come to having an obsession is football and while I might credibly be thought of as exuding a certain ageing hippy aura, small children and old ladies do not run from me in the street. It seems to me, however, that the possibility of God existing is of such importance and interest that it merits a lot of my attention. Since, manifestly, God's existence or non-existence cannot be either definitively proved or disproved (or the issue would have been settled by now and books like this would be redundant) questions about God do not go away simply because I have reached certain provisional conclusions about them. Similarly, the understanding of God found in Christian theology and the practices that emerge from this understanding are not mathematical formulae that I can follow and apply with absolute certainty. They, too, require continual examination, challenge and refinement.

The Three Legged Stool: Reason, Intuition and Experience

Quite quickly in my initial re-assessment of 'the God question', I recognised that an examination of God's existence and significance is not a matter simply of marshalling rational arguments for and against certain propositions. Reason is, of course, essential for any such examination, but I believe that we fool ourselves if we think that our decisions on 'ultimate questions' are based purely on reason. If this were so, it ought to be possible to come to a universally agreed, rational position on the question of God's existence. Many authors have attempted such a feat and, in my opinion, they have failed comprehensively. There is a plethora of books that have tried to demonstrate that the only truly rational position is either to believe or to disbelieve in the existence of God. In the main, it seems to me, their authors ignore the fact that life is made up of much more than rational thought processes, even though the irrational passion with which they sometimes write ought to give them a clue that such is the case.

My own experience of life indicates that, in practice, most, if not all, people tend to draw from personal 'reservoirs' when called upon to make really important decisions. These reservoirs contain such elements as reason, personal experience, psychological disposition, analytical aptitude, aesthetic appreciation, family background, spirituality and peer influences, all mixed together and seasoned with varying quantities of gut-feeling. This does not mean that rational argument is worthless, but it does suggest that I ought to recognise that while reason might provide a basis for decision-making, seldom does it *dictate* the actual decisions that I or others make. Of course, many writers and speakers may deny that they are driven by anything other than pure reason; I remain to be convinced. Belief in the absolute power of one's rationality might, perhaps, appropriately be called 'The Self Delusion'.

There is also a principled, rational objection to the assertion that reason is the only or always the primary way of understanding reality. Reason and the allied 'scientific method' of repeatable, verifiable experimentation and observation have rendered wonderful insights into the workings of the universe, but there is no valid rational argument for insisting that reason and the scientific method are the *only* ways of understanding and appreciating reality. I, along with the rest of the human race, simply do not know what all of reality *is* and there is no defensible way in which I can state that what we humans can observe scientifically forms *all* of reality: this would be an unwarranted and foolishly dogmatic assertion. Similarly, there is no defensible rational argument for stating that reason is the only *or even the primary* way of accessing *all aspects* of reality; *experience* and *intuition* also play important roles in enabling me to form an understanding of reality.

In certain instances, no amount of scientific evidence or rational argument can be a satisfactory substitute for *personal experience* even though rational argument and scientific evidence will often help me to understand my experiences and, in particular, help me to rule out certain unsustainable interpretations that I might otherwise attribute to them. For example, neither reason nor scientific evidence can give me an experience or a personal understanding of love. They can help me to understand some of the biological and psychological factors involved, but they can neither give me an experience of love nor can they provide anything like a comprehensive explanation of love; certainly not one that comes close to what I gain from actually experiencing it. What is more, there is no valid reason to suggest that they ought to be able to do so. On what basis might I argue that reason and science can explain everything, or even that they can explain *anything* exhaustively outside, perhaps, the spheres of mathematics and logic? None, I suggest, other than on dogmatic assumption. Even apparently physical things such as galaxies or molecules may not be *fully* understood simply because neither science nor the human mind has sufficient capacity to achieve that goal. When it comes to looking at *all* of reality, I must recognise, therefore, that some facets of it might only be accessible via personal experience.

Similarly, intuition, while not necessarily being opposed to either reason or science, does not always sit easily with them. By intuition, I mean an appreciation of reality that comes from a '*sense* of what is' even though this appreciation may not be either scientifically verifiable or rationally provable. Intuition covers everything from the vague feelings that prompt people to act in certain ways throughout their daily lives to the type of deep spiritual reflection found in meditation. For example, I gain an insight into reality by listening to music; one that I cannot gain in any other way. The same is true of art and of some aspects of nature. While science might be able to explain how music affects my brain, it cannot explain how or why it often gives rise to certain insights into my self-understanding or into my appreciation of the nature of human relationships. Again, there is no reason to believe that science ought to be able to do so.

Current insights from neuroscience indicate that in the human brain there is a genuine contrast between the left and right hemispheres with regard to the ways in which they deal with information. The left side of the brain is analytical, seeking to provide 'concrete' interpretations of reality. The right side of the brain is intuitive, seeking to provide holistic interpretations of reality. The left side looks at detail and processes; the right side looks at the 'big picture' and whole systems. The left side helps us to draw a map; the right side to paint a landscape. We need both sides of our brains to work in tandem to enable us to find a full appreciation of reality; there is, as far as I can tell, no *scientific* justification for arguing that the left, rational, side of our brains ought to have precedence over the right, intuitive side.

A version of one of 'Zeno's paradoxes' might help to illustrate the sort of problems that I might encounter if I were to insist that I ought always to rely primarily on reason in understanding the world around me. If I am standing at the side of a road and wish to get to the other side, I know both from experience and from intuition that all I need to do is to be certain that the road is sufficiently free from traffic and then to walk across. I know that, in the absence of some catastrophe, I shall easily cross the road. If, however, I decide to approach the task analytically, I might reflect that in order to cross the road I shall, first of all, have to walk halfway across it. To do so will take me some time, perhaps half the time that I think I would take to cross the whole road. I might then further reflect that in order to walk halfway across the road I shall, first of all, have to cross one quarter way across the road. This too shall take some time to complete. Letting the left side of my brain run riot, I might then realise that I could sub-divide the road into an infinite number of points that lie between me and the far side of the road, each of which will take some time to reach. An infinite number of points, each of which requires some time to reach, will mean that I shall take an infinitely long time to cross the road; in fact, because I have an infinite number of points to reach, I shall never reach the other side! This, of course, is nonsense and even the most analytical of thinkers do not stand fretting at the side of roads wondering how to get to the other side. It does, however, illustrate what can happen if we fall into the trap of relying on the rational side of our brains alone. At the very least, the above conundrum is *difficult* to resolve rationally in a manner that all will accept (some philosophers still question whether mathematicians have, comprehensively, resolved Zeno's paradoxes). From the aspects of intuition and experience, there is no problem at all; generations of human beings have been confident in their road-crossing abilities, centuries before mathematicians told them why this was possible.

Of course, personal experience and intuition are insufficient, in and of themselves, to enable me to understand reality; I need reason and I need science to help me gain a fuller and more balanced view of reality, even if a complete understanding of reality might, forever, be beyond my grasp. Reason, experience and intuition are like three interlocking circles, each with its own discreet area of insight but sharing overlapping areas with the others. I can see no valid reason for choosing only one way of understanding reality or for arguing that one method can give me access to all of reality. In order to do so, I should have to decide, in principle and without compelling empirical evidence, that I know essentially what reality is and that I also know that it may be accessed only or primarily in a particular way. This represents, not reasoned argument, but dogmatism. I need to be aware that fundamentalism comes in all shapes and sizes and that religion does not have a monopoly on it!

I think, however, that I need to go still further in recognising the limits that ought to be placed on rational thought as a means of deciding whether or not God exists. Were God to exist, it would be reasonable to suggest that God might want us to know that such was the case and, perhaps, God would also wish to have some sort of relationship with us. Given that some human beings have more limited abilities in abstract thinking and in employing rational thought than others, it would also be reasonable to suggest that God would not make rational thought the only, or perhaps even the primary, way in which some human beings would think of, or relate to, God. Intuition and experience will not only be important means by which some individuals may 'access' God, but if God were to be fair (as, again, it is reasonable to suggest that God might be), then intuition and experience must be *valid* means by which some people may come to believe in God; just as valid as the pathway of reason. It seems to me that if God exists, then access to God ought to be available to someone with very limited mental capacity; just as available, indeed, as to an intellectual genius. Such could not be the case if reason were always a *primary* means of 'accessing' God. While rational thought will continue to play an important role for most people in coming to an opinion with regard to God's existence, there are good grounds for believing that for some others it may play little or no role at all and that this is entirely appropriate.

In a similar vein, if God exists, I think that it is reasonable to suppose that God would wish God's existence to be accessible to people of every culture at every stage of human history. I must, therefore, be careful not to fall into the trap of thinking that God's existence or non-existence ought to be settled on the basis of scientific or other knowledge known only in the twenty-first century. This means that God ought to be 'accessible' to people used to employing very different patterns of thought, argument and exploration from those employed by me as someone living in a 'scientific age' (albeit sprinkled with post-modernism), as a member of a largely secular liberal democracy. To put it bluntly, I think that it is reasonable to suppose that, *if* it is a reality, God's existence ought to be as accessible to an ancient Egyptian slave or to a medieval English serf as it is to me. Clearly, if God does exist, God has quite a tall order to meet.

The ways in which reason, experience and intuition interact, sometimes complementing one another and sometimes appearing to be in conflict, are themes that, I suspect, will recur frequently in the course of this book. Partly because of my own predispositions and partly because atheism often seems to be based on a particular stream of rational thinking, I tend to begin with a rational approach to any given subject and then refine or correct it, where appropriate, in the light of experience or intuition. In a way, this *does* give rational thought a kind of priority, but I think that this is acceptable in the context of this book and similar enquiries. As long as I remind myself that experience and intuition ought to be given priority in certain situations, that for some people they are almost always to the fore and that I need to use them to 'check' my thinking, then I believe that my approach is defensible.

Why Christian Theology?

Given my experiences of life as a nineteen year old, firmly embedded within the Christian tradition, it is understandable that my initial examination of the issue of God's existence was based on Christian theology. I was a very active and committed Christian who had embraced a Christian way of thinking for as long as I could remember. Somewhat to my occasional surprise, I have remained, to date, an active and committed Christian, though I have to say that my understanding of what 'Christian' means has expanded considerably in the intervening years.

To be truthful, I am often ambivalent about the use of the term 'Christian'. So much negative history is associated with the term and so much questionable philosophy, theology and ethics attach to it that I frequently wish that a different word could be found. At the same time, I recognise that I am part of the historic stream of thought and life that emanated from the life of Jesus of Nazareth and I feel that to abandon the term would be both dishonest and disloyal. To indicate that what I am exploring is *my* understanding of theology, though obviously indebted to the Christian Church and to its many theologians, I shall italicize the word *Christian*. Others are free to agree with, to criticise, or to disown my musings as they wish; I am not claiming to represent anything or anyone other than myself.

Prior to beginning to write this book, my choice of continuing to believe in a *Christian* understanding of God has been based on an assessment that this provides a better explanation for, and appreciation of, reality than other options available to me, including atheism. As far as I have been aware (though, of course, *I* could be self-deluded), this assessment has been grounded in reason and seasoned by experience and intuition in much the same way as are all my important beliefs. I certainly do not want to give the impression that I do not appreciate the many insights of atheists or the varied perspectives found in other religions; I most definitely do. For reasons that I shall make clear later, however, up to this point my understanding of God has included such concepts as 'communal personality' and 'embodiment'. As such, the *Christian* doctrines of Trinity and Incarnation sit within what I have considered to be a reasonable and defensible understanding of God and this understanding 'absorbs' and expands other monotheistic interpretations of God. Of course, Jews, Muslims and other non-Christian monotheists will almost certainly disagree with this and I do not want to disparage or to belittle them (or anyone else) in any way. It still seems to me, however, that a *Christian* understanding of God is a 'comprehensive' form of monotheism and, as such, it deserves first examination. Of course, if the ideas of God being Trinity or God becoming incarnate are shown to be either absurd or false (or both), then other monotheistic theories may still be pursued.

Similarly, while I recognise that I am often psychologically drawn to the concept of an impersonal God, I find that a 'communal-personality' understanding of God is more challenging. As such, while some of the insights to be found in Buddhism and some other Eastern religions are not necessarily negated by insights found in a *Christian* understanding of God, they are superseded by them. Polytheism is, of course, incompatible with monotheism and if God is a 'communal-personality' rather then a multiple of persons, then polytheism falls by the wayside.

To date, my cycles of examination and re-examination of the God-question have led me to believe that a qualified *Christian* understanding of God is most likely to be correct and, so far, that is where I have pitched my theological tent. It is an approach that has contributed positively to my life although I acknowledge that my appreciation of what a *Christian* understanding of God might entail tends to expand with each successive cycle of examination. I am not sure what a nineteen year-old version of me would have made of the beliefs that I now hold as a fifty-something *Christian* theist, but then, truth to be told, I am more interested in what a sixty or seventy-something version of me might believe in the future.

In the rest of this book, I intend to embark openly on another cycle of enquiry, re-examining the God-question. I am not trying to convince anyone, including myself, of anything and, if I end up coming to different conclusions from the ones that I have hitherto reached then I shall simply see where that takes me. Truth to be told, I shall be rather disappointed if I end up with exactly the same beliefs that I started out with; it seems to me that if that were to happen, I will not have done very much exploring. I am not, of course, starting with a clean slate; that would be an impossibility and it would be disingenuous of me to claim to be able to do so. I can only begin with whom and with what I am. This, I hope, will not stop me from attempting a genuine re-examination of *Christian* theology. I recognise that many of my previous explorations were underpinned by a desire to *affirm belief*; in this examination, I am deliberately eschewing such an approach. I am adamant that this will be a genuine enquiry, *examining* issues of belief; it will not be an exercise in defending or bolstering belief. While past experience has led me into continued belief, I cannot be certain where this particular cycle will lead. I shall attempt to be as honest as possible, also recognising that on some levels I find atheism a more attractive option than belief, but I shall try not to let this, or any other, bias affect my enquiry.

In examining 'God issues' I will be pursuing three main goals. My starting point is to see whether or not the existence of God is a *plausible* idea (is there room in the universe for God?). If my understanding of the nature of reality is not *compatible* with belief in God's existence, then atheism will be the only option open to me. If, however, a compatible understanding can be found, then I shall wish to explore, from a *Christian* perspective, what 'sort of God' might exist and what might be some of the implications of God's existence (can I 'make sense' of God?). Up to this point in my life, I have concluded that a *Christian* understanding of God is, *in principle*, tenable, but, again, I shall see where this current enquiry leads me. Finally, if both of these quests are successful, I will look at the question of whether or not *actual belief* in God as understood in *Christian* theology might be credible (might God be real?).

I recognise that my way of exploring a *Christian* view of God will, inevitably, be different from the ways in which others would go about making similar enquiries. This book, however, represents a *personal* enquiry; it is not a textbook. I make no pretence, therefore, of adopting a neutral or disinterested tone. This examination is deeply personal to me and I hope that my engagement with the God question will benefit, not suffer, from my taking this stance.

Equally, because this is a genuine quest, I hope that this will spur me on to ensure that I shall leave no stones unturned in my investigation. That, at least, is my intention.

Chapter Two

What's the Matter? – The Attraction of Materialism
(Recognising Prejudices… The Nature of the Physical Universe… The Possibility that Non-Physical Things Exist)

Recognising Prejudices

As I begin to examine whether or not belief in the existence of God is compatible with a considered understanding of reality, I have to acknowledge, first of all, some prejudices that I find difficult to shift. I have come to realise that one of the factors that encourages me to be an atheist by inclination, is the way in which 'cultural atheism' suggests that it is the only intelligent option for people who are prepared to think seriously about life. I don't want to be gullible; more than that, in spite of my general tendency not to care very much about what others think of me, I have to confess that I don't really want to be *thought of* as being gullible. Partly as a defence mechanism, therefore, I incline towards scepticism which makes atheism seem an attractive option. In truth, I also recognise that scepticism seems to be my default mode, no doubt for a variety of psychological as well as intellectual reasons. I find it difficult not to challenge whatever might be the perceived wisdom on any given topic. This, I appreciate, makes me a rather exhausting and, at times, irritating person to know, but I have such a deep suspicion of any 'herd instinct' and such an abhorrence of mob-mentality that I am prepared to put up with the inconvenience of wearing thin other people's patience. In my defence, I cannot help but think that if a healthy dose of scepticism had been embraced by the Christian Church down through the centuries such abominations as heresy trials and witch-hunts would never have happened.

In addition, I am wary of many religious people; not so of much 'average' church-goers, but of those who claim some sort of expertise in the realms of faith. They can be, to put it at its mildest, a bit weird. I tend to like people and things that are unconventional so I am not against 'weirdness' in and of itself, but *some* Christians (the religious group that I am most acquainted with) strike me as being weird in a particularly irritating way as well as being more than a tad gullible. Many insist in using incomprehensible jargon, some inhabit a sub-culture that ties them to the utterances of celebrity preachers regardless of the preposterous nature of some of their pronouncements; some eschew vast swathes of ordinary life in favour of immersion in the activities of closed and, frankly, rather incestuous groups. I am constantly bemused by people who are articulate, intelligent and enquiring in all areas of their lives other than in the area of faith where they resemble not very inquisitive five year olds, prepared to believe whatever they are told they ought to believe, without question and without examination. There are so many tests of orthodoxy (many of them contradictory) that it is a full-time occupation recognising, never mind passing, them. I have some difficulty deciding which makes me feel more uncomfortable: the thought of being gullible or the thought of being associated with groups that get worked up over arcane liturgical practices (who cares?) or who attend endless ';inspirational' conferences (who could be bothered?) or who hotly debate such topics as the timing of end of the world (who knows?) In truth, in my cycles of examination and re-examination of Christian theology, I have been through most, if not all, such groups and while I gratefully take much with me from my experiences, I also wince with embarrassment at some of the things that I allowed myself to be badgered into believing or practising in order to be 'accepted'; happily a pursuit I no longer follow. The Christian mafia comes in all guises, but each variety, in my experience, insists on absolute loyalty to its particular creeds and codes of practice.

I feel that I need to point out that in all honesty, I am not as grumpy as the above paragraph makes me appear. Indeed, I am not really a grumpy person at all, but I can do without much of the sheer tedium and irrelevance that seems to fill the lives and claim the attention of many Christians. The weirdness of some Christians, the pre-occupation of many Christians with things that are peripheral to the experiences and concerns of most ordinary people, the desire to be sheltered from the realities of life: these all combine, with an unspoken assumption that sensible, intelligent people do not fall for pie in the sky, to produce within me an emotional and psychological atheism.

I think that it is important for me to acknowledge this and to recognise the influence that it might have on any attempts that I make to investigate Christian thought. I admit that I often have to make a deliberate effort to get beyond Christian groups in order to look fairly at Christian belief. Truthfully, I find many Christians interesting and some even delightful as individuals, but when too many of them (us!) get together, I frequently find myself wanting to be in other company. I can't take seriously the pomp of some formal rituals (I often want to giggle) or the self-importance of some charismatic pronouncements (I often want to scream). I despair that, in my experience, church politics are just as cut throat and as self-serving as any other kind of politics.

In short, everything in me militates against being involved in organised Christianity – apart from the undoubted benefits that come from those churches and groups that are prepared to get their hands dirty in taking a stand for social justice. True, I can appreciate church services if they form a spiritual focal point for an authentic community or if, as acts of worship, they genuinely seek to encourage awareness of God (if God exists) rather than self-aggrandisement. Conversely, I respond very negatively to anything that appears to use worship or the desire of people to express faith or devotion as an opportunity for self-promotion on the part of clergy, choirs, worship bands or ecclesiastical dignitaries. That is who and what I am. I don't argue that anyone else ought to react in similar ways, that they ought to agree with me, or even that they ought to like me. I simply need to recognise that this is part of the baggage that I bring with me when, in the context of Christianity, I explore the question of God's existence.

All of this, of course, I need to acknowledge and then 'park' as I examine whether I can consider belief in God to be viable. To be fair, I must admit that the Church, for all its faults, has done no worse and probably has done better than many other organisations. Schools, hospitals and social welfare movements owe much to churches as well as to individual Christians, so I suppose I must not be too hard on organised Christianity or, at least, on all parts of it. (Those of a certain generation might, at this point, recall Monty Python's 'What have the Romans ever done for us?' sketch). Neither the merits nor demerits of Christians and churches are determining factors, however, in deciding whether or not God exists; it is important, though, that I recognise my biases and prejudices from the outset.

Not wishing to be gullible, or wanting to be associated with many forms and expressions of Christianity has made it natural for me to adopt atheism as my 'default' philosophical starting point. I also have to add to this, my personal experiences of some Christians and Christian groups that suggest, sadly, that confession of Christian faith can be a useful way of deflecting attention from some ethically questionable practices. All in all, I find very little to attract me psychologically or emotionally to organised Christianity and so, I gravitate towards atheism. It is, of course, intellectually indefensible to allow these thoughts to impinge on my examination of whether or not God exists; just as intellectually indefensible as pre-supposing theism to be true. I know, rationally, that I ought to begin with some form of principled agnosticism, but I have to struggle to get there. My rational mind may tell me that any investigation into the possibility of God's existence ought to start on a level playing field, but, to mix my metaphors, I know that, *psychologically*, I start with the dice loaded in favour of atheism. I also need to explore if, intellectually as well as psychologically, this might also be the case.

The Physical Universe

It has taken me some years to realise that whenever the topic of God's existence crops up in conversation, I have an inbuilt intellectual bias towards believing that the correct starting point for any such discussion ought to be atheism. In other words, I automatically assume that the onus is on those who believe in God's existence to prove their case rather than on atheists to prove theirs. I have to ask myself, however, why this should be the case, since agnosticism would appear to be a better starting point. After all, I am open-minded about many other things that are invisible and intangible. The history of philosophy shows that atheism is not so self-evidently obvious that it deserves to be accepted intellectually as the only proper starting point for any discussion on the possibility of God's existence. Neither is it the case that postulating the existence of God is so manifestly absurd that it deserves to be laughed out of court. Many theories that suggest that God exists are philosophically sophisticated; believing in God's existence is not like believing in the Man in the Moon. Why then, when someone asks if belief in God is reasonable, do I still tend to start with the premise that God does not exist rather than starting with an open mind?

The main reason, I believe, is science or, to put it more accurately, a particular perception of science and the role that it has in modern life and thought. It is not just that some well-known scientists are aggressively atheistic and delight in giving the impression that no one with even half a brain cell could possibly believe in God. That is really just part of the cultural and psychological pressure that I feel to be an atheist and needs simply to be put to one side. Once people start claiming that those who disagree with them lack either intelligence or integrity it is time to move swiftly on; such comments invariably say more about those that make them than they do about those against whom they are directed. Nonetheless, there can be no escaping the common perception that science makes belief in God untenable; this in spite of the fact that there are many scientists who are theists. While what I have said in the previous chapter about the importance of experience and intuition remains true, it is also the case that the challenge of popular science needs to be faced. In asking whether or not my understanding of reality might be compatible with belief in the existence of God, I need to look carefully at the impact that science might have in shaping my view of reality.

This is an issue that must be grappled with, even if, as I suspect, the thread of the argument might, at times, become a bit convoluted. Scientists and non-scientists, philosophers and non-philosophers alike, appear to be incapable of agreeing on the meaning of some of the terms that occur in debates about God and this does not lend itself to tidiness of thought. I confess that I love reading books and articles on theoretical physics, but I also have to admit that I am unable to follow more than the most elementary formulae and equations; my grasp of mathematics simply is not up to the task. What compels me to keep on reading though, are the philosophical and theological implications of what physicists discuss. Theirs is a universe (or universes) of complexity, subtlety and boundless potential. Their grasp of reality is, at times, breathtaking, putting into the shade the offerings of many theologians. Their explorations also serve as a warning to anyone who insists that reality is plain and simple and that it can be reduced to what we can readily see, touch, measure and quantify.

This, it seems to me, is a key issue, since the perception that abounds in many circles is that scientists understand enough about the universe to state confidently that the fundamental 'stuff' (a favourite technical term of physicists and philosophers) of the universe is matter/energy and that 'physical materialism' is the only viable backdrop against which any theory of life may correctly be formulated. By 'physical materialism' I mean any theory that considers matter/energy to consist of observable, measurable 'material' such as atoms, protons, quarks and so on and that ultimately and fundamentally, that is *all* that there is to reality. There is nothing more or less to life, the universe and everything than matter/energy and this is, in principle, entirely open to scientific verification. This perception is widely held among many non-scientists and scientists alike, although it is only fair to point out that a significant number of scientists are much less certain of this assertion than are many non-scientists who believe that this is what science 'teaches'. Nonetheless, if it is true, or if it can be demonstrated that it is the only viable theory to follow, then belief in God, and all subsequent faith and theology, ought to be discarded and I can return to my natural home of atheism.

Physical materialism makes bold assertions, but, in spite of its undoubted pull on me, I fail to find the theory persuasive. On the evidence of what we now know about the nature of the universe I have to conclude that any theory of physical materialism is based on a particular understanding of the matter/energy that we humans observe in, on and around our own planet. Such 'ordinary' matter, however, we now know comprises a mere five percent of the physical 'stuff' that makes up the universe. 'Dark matter' and 'dark energy' make up ninety five percent of the universe and, truth to be told, we know very little about them. Their composition, qualities and internal laws are almost entirely a mystery. There is, therefore, no proper rationale for basing my understanding of the universe on 'ordinary' matter; indeed, I ought to view the matter that scientists are used to observing as 'extraordinary' since it comprises such a small percentage of the universe. Just as cosmology was once geo-centric, but had to change radically to accommodate a fuller understanding of the Earth's place in the universe, so too physics which is currently centred on 'ordinary' matter/energy might have to make equally radical changes in the light of a fuller understanding of 'dark' matter and energy.

This alerts me to take seriously a thought that I and many others find difficult to swallow: there is absolutely no valid reason why human beings ought to think that we might ever understand the true nature and composition of the universe. We are strangely given to believe that just because we are human, we have some inherent right or innate ability to comprehend the nature of reality. Why should this be so? There are no grounds for making this astounding assumption; absolutely none at all. I and others like me might simply have to acknowledge, reluctantly, that our minds are much too small and much too limited fully to understand such things. Just because we think that we are super-intelligent it does not follow that we are! The fact that ninety-five percent of the universe is a mystery to us ought to encourage us, perhaps, to have a degree of humility and a due sense of the possible limits to our intelligence.

What is more, the closer physicists have looked at 'ordinary' matter, the less ordinary it seems to become. Once it has clumped itself into the relatively large building blocks that we call atoms (once thought to be the smallest particles in the universe) it behaves in a largely predictable and sensible fashion. At a sub-atomic level, however, there appears to be a potentially endless process of refinement of matter not only into smaller and smaller particles, but into 'stuff' that barely appears to be matter at all. Indeed, there is a real possibility that when matter is 'reduced' to its most elemental state, what exists in what physicists term a 'quantum vacuum' is an alternating state of being and non-being, dependant upon whether or not matter/energy is being observed. Ask physicists today to state what matter 'is' and they will admit that they don't really know. In fact, the quest to work out what matter 'is', to discover a Theory of Everything or a Grand Unified Theory, is the holy grail of physics and it is proving to be more elusive than anything that the knights of the Round Table ever faced in their epic struggles. 'Ordinary' matter, it seems, is not only extraordinary in terms of its prevalence in the universe, but it is also far from ordinary when scientists try to describe, never mind to define, it. How odd then, to assert as boldly as some do, that physical materialism is the only viable backdrop against which we can formulate an understanding of life.

What I think *is* defensible is to say, is that from our perspective within the universe we are able to observe, *at a certain level of organisation*, the existence of 'ordinary' matter; i.e. material that has mass and that occupies space (or, at least, appears to us to do so). Below this level of organisation, physical substances certainly exist but they become ever less and less like 'material'. Some of these substances seem to be able to be in two places at the same time, some appear to be able to affect each other *instantaneously* although separated by distance, while some of the behaviour of matter transformed into energy in the form of light seems to defy much of what we might expect from it.

If matter/energy becomes more and more intriguing as it is examined in detail, what might be said of other fundamentals of the observable universe that appear to be intrinsically related to it? Scientists are assured of the existence of gravity, electro-magnetism and strong and weak nuclear forces even if, once again, the exact nature of these fundamentals is far from certain. Gravity, in particular, has shown itself to be a particularly slippery customer, being much more complex as well as much more important for the formation and continued existence of the universe than Isaac Newton could ever have imagined when viewing his fabled apple. Einstein revolutionised physicists' understanding of gravity, but voices are now raised suggesting that his insights fail to describe adequately this most pervasive and yet most elusive of fundamental forces. It seems that the more scientists investigate matter/energy and other fundamentals in the universe the more they realise that they are still some way off being able to describe the properties of what they can observe, never mind the properties of the *entire* universe. In short, science can comment on what it can observe and it may theorise from these observations on what it cannot observe, but it cannot tell me very much, if anything, about what, in principle or in practice, is beyond its scope.

The Non-Physical Universe

The issue that presents itself to my mind as I examine whether or not science makes belief in God untenable is that of the possibility of there being *non-physical* 'stuff' in the universe. Two interesting aspects of the universe that I take for granted are not, in themselves, *physical*: space and time, or to put it more accurately, 'space-time' since physicists prefer to think of them as forming a single continuum enabling scientists to 'map' the universe, indicating the 'where' and the 'when' of everything from sub-atomic particles to galaxies. That space-time exists, few would dispute, but it is not made of anything physical. Space-time has no mass, energy, spin or momentum or any of the other features we associate with the physical. It is non-physical and yet, strange as it may seem, physicists are assured that space-time is subject to the effects of gravity. Of course, it may be argued that space-time depends on the existence of physical things for its existence: if there was no energy/matter there would be nothing to map and hence there would be no space-time map at all, but that does not alter the fact that the space-time map is both real and non-physical. Distance, for example is a measurement between two or more points, but what is it composed of? Time is a measurement between two or more events, but what is it?

Something similar might be said about mathematics or logic, both of which are real and non-physical. Fundamental mathematical laws underpin much of what physicists are able to understand of the nature of the physical universe. Were they not there, either the universe would not exist at all or it would be unintelligible at a fundamental level. Similarly, if laws of logic did not exist, we would be unable to discuss anything of import in a rational manner. Whether such laws are products of our brains or whether they are laws that exist independently from us does not affect the truth that they are both real and non-physical.

Even more striking, and more significant, candidates for the non-physical category are mental activity and 'mind'. By mental activity, I mean the full array of such things as thoughts, feelings, perceptions and reflective self-awareness or consciousness, the *amalgamation* of which is sometimes termed, 'mind'. Mind is not quite the same as thought, for example, but it may be considered to be thought-plus. The 'plus' is what may be viewed as an ability by an individual both to create a thought and to reflect on it as well as an ability to be aware of such reflection and of 'oneself' as both thinker and reflector. Many animals appear to be capable of having feelings and perceptions and some display an ability to think, all of which are mental activities, but as far as I know, none display reflective self-awareness, a key element in human consciousness. Just as the physical universe includes more than matter although matter is physical, mind includes more than thought although thought is a form of mental activity. The whole area of mind, I believe, deserves further exploration since it provides, at the very least, a significant challenge to physical materialism and, consequently, to an automatic acceptance of atheism.

Thoughts, feelings, perceptions and my awareness of them are non-physical in that they have absolutely no physical characteristics. For example, they do not have mass, they are not energy, they do not occupy space and they have no velocity. I cannot locate a particular thought in space (although I might be able to locate the *occurrence* of the thought in my brain) and say, 'there it is' and I cannot meaningfully say that my thoughts travel at a particular speed since thoughts don't physically travel anywhere (although electrical signals associated with thoughts *do* travel between neurons). I cannot measure my thoughts' weight, their length, their volume or their electro-magnetic charge. Even if I were able to watch a thought ('I fancy a glass of wine') occurring via sophisticated brain-imagery all I could say is that I saw the thought occurring but I did not see the thought itself since *thoughts* are not visible. Thoughts are known only to their thinkers and even if I were able to decode the electrical messages running between my neurons or if I were to decode the electro-magnetic field generated in my brain all I would have achieved would be to break down the mechanics of a thought, but not to capture the thought itself. Just as the words on this page *convey* a series of thoughts, but are not thoughts until someone reads them and thinks them, the electrical workings of my brains are not, in themselves thoughts: thoughts require a thinker.

Feelings are similar. The experience of pain or the feeling of love may be accompanied by, or even triggered by, a series of physiological processes, but these processes, themselves, are not feelings. Pain is felt by a conscious 'feeler'; love is experienced by a 'lover'. People have different pain-thresholds (and maybe love-thresholds as well) because they experience pain differently. The physiological processes are the same, but the *experience* is different. Even though, as I write this, I am well into my sixth decade, I still play football each week, although it is now of a somewhat stiff-limbed and indoor nature. Nonetheless, I play with as much intent, enthusiasm and competitiveness as I did when I was twenty years old. I frequently emerge with cuts and bruises that I barely notice, if at all, during the course of a game, but an hour later after having soaked in a bath, I invariably limp and moan my way into an armchair. The difference in my experience may, at one level, be explained by my brain chemistry, but this does not do justice to my experience. The pain-numbing chemicals are produced, in part at least, because during a football match, I am concentrating on the game itself whereas after bathing I afford myself the luxury of concentrating on my aches and pains. Similarly, if, having gone home and bathed, something suitably distracting was to command my attention, my aches and pains would soon disappear.

Perceptions are equally 'mental' and non-physical in their nature. Even what may seem to me to be the most obviously 'physical' of perceptions is far from being so. I might take, for example, looking at a piece of red paper. The paper seems to me to be red because that is how I perceive it, but 'redness' does not exist apart from my and other minds. The piece of paper absorbs and/or emits certain parts of the electro-magnetic spectrum, but there is nothing 'red' about those particular waves. If I or someone else were not present, looking at the paper, the 'red' would not exist; there would just be a piece of paper that absorbs or emits a particular part of the spectrum. Indeed, someone who is 'colour blind' might join me and say quite firmly that the piece of paper is brown. We could engage in a totally fruitless conversation, with me trying to prove that a certain part of the electro-magnetic spectrum is red and with him or her arguing that I am wrong and that the part of the spectrum that we are talking about is, in fact, brown. I might argue that I am able to subdivide the spectrum better than he or she is and that the subdivision that I am talking about is red and my companion could retort that I am quite wrong, that no such colour as 'red' exists because I can neither describe it nor show it to him or her in a way that does not appear to be brown.

Many other examples of thoughts, feelings and perceptions could be given, but the basic point that strikes me is that all of these, as well as my awareness of them, are non-physical. Clearly, 'higher' aspects of mind such as awareness, reasoning, intention and appreciation are similarly non-physical.

I find it reasonable to suggest, therefore, that in the universe both physical and non-physical things exist and among the non-physical things are mental activity and mind. Scientific enquiry can tell me something about the nature of physical things (although, as I have already suggested, scientists have to be guarded in their claims since they deal with only a small proportion of the material in the universe), but it is far from clear what it can tell me about the non-physical. At this point, at least, there is nothing in science that makes the idea of God (assuming that God is non-physical) obsolete or incongruous, but, of course, there is nothing, at this point, in science to suggest that the existence of God is a reality. In fact, at this juncture, science is entirely neutral; an observation worth noting in itself, but one which is often overlooked. Nonetheless, such a discussion of the physical and non-physical aspects of the universe, leads me inevitably to ask the question: how might the physical and the non-physical (in particular mental activity) *relate* to one another?

Chapter Three

Dual-Control? – The Relationship between Mind and Matter

(Theories of Reality: Physical Materialism, Dualism, Emergence…
the Nature of the Relationship between Brains and Minds)

Theories of Reality

In trying to tease out the relationship between the physical and the non-physical it seems reasonable to me to start with something that I know and experience for myself: my own body and mind. What I can observe or theorise with regard to myself I might then be able to apply to the bigger issue of the possible ways in which the physical and the mental may relate to one other, not only in other people, but also in the rest of the universe. In many articles, books and debates, this discussion is usually phrased in terms of a body/mind or brain/mind conundrum and it tends to focus on the nature of the relationship between brains and consciousness.

While I am aware that there are almost endless refinements of the positions I am about to outline, in my judgement, theories of the relationship between brains and minds can be focused on three basic theories. These are: physical materialism (our brains and minds are fully one and the same), dualism (our brains and minds belong to two totally different categories, each with its own independent source and existence) and emergence (brains give rise to minds, but brains and minds are not one and the same thing). As I have said, refinements abound, but these are the main contenders in providing insight into how the physical and the mental might relate to one another in human experience.

In the interest of brevity (and sanity) I am choosing to put to one side 'fringe' theories such as those that state that experiences like reading this book are illusions or that I am really a character in someone else's dream or that nothing at all exists apart from my mind and that everything else, including this book, is a product of my personal imagination. It is not that these and similar teasers do not have a certain twisted appeal; it's just that life is too short to spend time exploring them outside the realms of fiction. I am going to run with the proposition that *in all probability*, my intuition is correct and that I and other human beings are real people with brains and minds (or brain/minds). Of course, if any of the more exotic theories is true, there would be no point in continuing with this book, or indeed with anything at all; I ought simply to dream on.

That there are both physical and non-physical/mental aspects to my life seems, to me, to be beyond reasonable doubt. I cut my finger with a knife and it bleeds; a very physical occurrence. I think to myself, 'Be more careful in future' (or words to that effect) and a very non-physical event has taken place. The former occurred and is full of space-time 'measurables' involving everything from sharp metal implements to intricate biochemical processes. The latter also occurred, but it can not be measured, observed, weighed or even accurately located (the *occurrence* of the thought may be susceptible to some of these measurements, but the thought itself, is not.). Both the event and its accompanying thought are real; the question is, how, if at all, are they related?

Physical Materialism

If I were a physical materialist I would first of all argue that having cut my finger, my brain somehow gave rise not only to the thought that followed, but also to my awareness of that thought. I would then insist that my cut finger, the thought that I ought to be more careful in future and my awareness of thinking that thought are all purely physical events. They are not only the *products* of physical processes that may be understood at a variety of levels including biochemical or sub-atomic levels, but they are to be *identified* completely with those physical processes; there is no essential distinction to be made between any of them.

In truth, if I were to adopt physical materialism I should have to accept that there is no 'I' that thinks or that is aware of 'me' thinking at all; such thoughts must be banished along with belief in Santa Claus and the Tooth Fairy. All that happens when 'I' think is that a complicated bio-chemical entity, built up inexorably from sub-atomic particles, through a series of processes set in motion from the first moments of the universe following the 'Big Bang', has conformed to the physical laws that govern the universe. The fact that 'I' think that 'I' have thought anything is a mirage; after all, there is no 'I'.

This, frankly, is too much for me to take. It requires me to put too much faith in a hypothesis that is not only deeply counter-intuitive but one that, in principle, can never be properly examined, never mind proved. In order for me to explore the possibility that I am nothing more than the sum total of physical processes, I must act as if I am, in fact, more than the sum total of physical processes and hence able to think, to reason and to engage in genuine exploration. If, however, my thinking and reasoning can be reduced completely to physical processes, then I am not really thinking or reasoning at all, I am simply part of a series of physical interactions. The series of physical interactions that I am part of will be different from the series of physical interactions that someone else will be part of and, consequently, we may come to different conclusions about the theory of physical materialism. Of course, 'we' would not have come to any conclusions at all; 'we' would simply have conformed to whatever physical interactions were going on in 'our' brains. Physical materialism asks me to sacrifice any belief that 'I' exist as a personal being without providing compelling evidence to support its contention. Indeed, if it were to be true, physical materialism demands that I accept that everything that I think and do, including writing this book, ought to be seen as nothing more than an outworking of physical laws that leave no room for choice, freedom, intention or even rational thought. It is important, I believe, to realise that this is precisely where physical materialism leads and that, indeed, that it can only lead to this destination.

If I were to assume that everything not only conforms to physical laws and processes but also that nothing else apart from these laws and processes does or can exist, then, in principle, everything that exists is both physical and determined. That is to say, through a vast array of interactions, each conforming to physical laws, everything will act in predictable and determined ways. The end result of this, in the example given above, is that at a certain time and place a finger that is part of the physical entity labelled 'Brendan McCarthy' was cut and the brain of the same physical entity underwent a series of internal interactions resulting from this external stimulus that may be decoded as transmitting the information 'Be more careful in future' (although it is unclear to whom this information was transmitted). Everything from the Big Bang to that coded message has conformed to physical laws and processes. Given the initial conditions of the Big Bang, the cutting of a finger at a certain time and place, along with everything else between this event and the Big Bang, happened because they *had* to happen: physical laws and processes indicate that such must be the case. Even the introduction of uncertainty at a sub-atomic level, accepted by physicists, does not change this scenario very much: uncertainty at a sub-atomic level does not seem to be significant once matter has formed itself into atomic size particles and I am significantly larger than an atom.

I really cannot see how embracing physical materialism can avoid the conclusion that everything is physically determined; hence there are no such things as choice, free-will, intention, decision-making or even rational thought. I am writing this book, exploring and espousing my thoughts, not because they have any logical, psychological or philosophical worth, but simply because this is what physical laws have indicated that my brain ought to do at this particular time. Anyone reading this book is doing so because of the interplay of similar processes and any thoughts or reflections that he or she might have are not *really* thoughts or reflections but biochemical processes that are better thought of as parcels of information generated and transported by his or her brain. There is no *reason* why these events are happening, other than the inevitable outplaying of impersonal processes. There is no point to any of it, no 'value' or 'meaning'; something that some popular scientific writers mask by introducing statements such as 'nature intends' or 'genes decide'. In physical materialism no one and nothing intends or decides anything.

Physical materialism leads me to conclude that, contrary to my experience of everyday life, I am really nothing other than a collection of particles acting in predetermined ways. Somehow, although it is impossible to understand how or why, some physical collections in the universe (human beings among them) have, developed a false sense of personal consciousness that includes such mistaken concepts as intention, decision-making and rational thought. Such things do not exist at all in the universe of the physical materialist; they are all mirages.

Far from being contested, this 'realisation' has led some scientists to affirm that consciousness does, indeed, not exist, that 'persons' do not exist and that all intellectual activity is nothing more that the interaction of physical processes. This means that it is utterly impossible to tell whether anything is right or wrong or even whether anything actually exists since all that we 'experience' is the interplay of matter/energy. If physical materialism is true, then *there is no way of actually knowing if it is true*, since there is no-one and nothing to check its validity. I might 'think' that I can check its claims and others might 'believe' that they can do so too, but all that is happening is that the physical laws and processes of the universe are continuing their inexorable progress which will include, for a short period of time, collecting matter and energy into forms of life that mistakenly think that they can think.

There is, of course, no way of disproving physical materialism; as with all belief systems, its proponents are able to interpret all data, scientific and otherwise, in such a way that it will conform to their chosen theory. At the same time, it is equally evident that there is no demonstrable way of proving that it is true. It is based on an *assumption* that all that exists is matter/energy, understood to be entirely physical and conforming to entirely physical laws, and that nothing other than this does or can exist. Espousing this theory is, as I have already suggested, counter-productive in that if it is true there is no such thing as personal thought and therefore no basis for making the assumption in the first place. Physical materialism might be true, but there are no grounds for *insisting* that such is the case. If I believe, *intuitively*, that my experience of feeling, will, intention, rational thought and other non-physical events and experiences are real, then I have good reason for questioning the validity of physical materialism and for looking elsewhere for a better understanding of the relationship between the physical and the mental in human experience. It seems to me that the claims and the implications of physical materialism are such that the burden of proof must lie with its proponents. To date I have not encountered any arguments to cause me to abandon my belief that physical materialism fails sufficiently to explain my *experience* of being a person with feelings, thought, will and intention even though, from time to time, a part of me wishes that such were the case so that I could lapse into a deterministic disregard for my actions and their consequences.

Dualism

Dualism stands in stark and complete contrast to physical materialism. Dualists believe that the brain and the mind represent two separate types of existence; two distinct categories of being. Just as matter can only be understood in physical terms, building in complexity from sub-atomic particles all the way through to advanced life-forms, so too, mind can only be understood in non-physical or mental terms. Dualism, it seems, comes in many shapes and sizes with numerous refinements of the basic theory that the physical and the mental are separate categories of being, but they all agree that 'mind' is real and that it cannot be explained by, or reduced to, any form of physical explanation.

As with physical materialism, there is no way in which to disprove dualism. Many attempts to do so tend to rely on its opponents pouring scorn on there being 'ghosts in the machine', suggesting that dualism belongs to a pre-scientific age when ghosts, goblins and spirits were to be seen at work just about everywhere. Such visceral attacks on dualism, it seems to me, prove nothing and account for very little in trying to work out how the brain and the mind relate to one another. As a theory, dualism, in one form or another, has been espoused by many philosophers throughout the history of the human race and still has its advocates today. If the price I have to pay for believing that physical materialism is true is a denial or thought, will and intention and if dualism were the only alternative theory available to me, then I should prefer dualism since, at the very least, it takes seriously the existence and the integrity of both the physical and mental aspects of human life.

Nevertheless, there are serious problems associated with dualism, or at least with the sort of 'pure' dualism that I have outlined above. If my brain and my mind belong to two quite separate realms, how can they relate to one another? One answer proposed by some dualists is that they don't and that any correlation between a thought and a physical event is simply that: a correlation and not a cause-and-effect sequence or even an event in which one has influenced the other.

This, it appears to me, flies in the face both of intuition and experience. My experience of life suggests that a two-way street operates between thoughts and physical events. To return to my cut finger; the wound triggers a series of physiological events that culminate in brain-activity that registers the cut and the damage that it has inflicted on my body. This, in turn results in me *experiencing* pain; itself a non-physical event which, in turn, causes me to reflect (albeit, very briefly) on the undesirability of having a cut finger and I come to the conclusion that I ought to be more careful in future, thus affecting my future behaviour. From the manifestly physical event of a sharp piece of metal cutting my skin to the non-physical event of my concluding thought and its subsequent implications, there is clearly a pathway. It is true that the pathway is not entirely a simple cause-and-effect one since I could have come to a different conclusion with regard to my future actions, perhaps not caring if I were to cut myself again or even finding it a pleasurable experience, but a pathway of some sort clearly exists. While the *content* of my final thought is not *caused* by my experience of pain, my non-physical *experience* of pain *is* caused by my physical experience of receiving a cut and a final thought of some sort is an inevitable consequence of the pain that I experienced. If a simple linear cause and effect sequence cannot always be shown to exist between physical and non-physical events, the physical and the non-physical are linked in some effectual way in that if one thing had not happened (a cut finger) another (the thought to be more careful in the future) would not have occurred.

The street, as I have said, runs in both directions. As I am sitting writing this, I have been aware for some time that I would like a cup of coffee. I have resisted this non-physical thought, initiated, perhaps, by some physiological promptings associated with caffeine withdrawal and I have continued to type this manuscript. I am aware, however, that my desire to continue typing is not so strong that pausing to go into my kitchen to make a cup of coffee ought to be put off much longer. In order to demonstrate to myself that my decision to stop typing and to go and make myself a cup of coffee is governed neither by physiological promptings nor by some other physical trigger mechanism in my brain, I am now deciding that I shall stop typing in exactly three minutes and fifteen seconds from now; a time that I have arbitrarily chosen by sticking a pin in a list of times that I have written out on a piece of paper (I really do need to get out more). When my alarm goes off, I shall stop typing even if I am in the middle of a word and rise and go into the kitchen. At that point, a non-physical *thought* about the desirability of drinking a cup of coffee, which I turned into a non-physical *decision* to go and make a cup of coffee, will have the effect of a flurry of brain activity resulting in my muscles contracting and expanding in order for me to rise from my chair. Other areas of brain activity, accompanied, no doubt by caffeine-associated thoughts, will enable me to navigate my way out of my study, into the kitchen, enabling me to conduct the arduous task of boiling the kettle and so forth.

By coincidence, the alarm went off just as I finished the above paragraph and I am now sitting at my computer, armed with a mug of coffee. However this little drama may be described, it is clear that non-physical events (thoughts) resulted in physical events (rising, walking, making a cup of coffee, etc). The problem for a 'pure' dualist (as well as for a physical materialist) is to explain how my brain and my mind managed to interact in the ways in which they did.

Of course, a dualist might simply answer that he or she does not know; that, indeed, the mechanism for such interactions might never be known but that it is probable that the brain has something to do with it. Again, I think that it is worth saying that if the only alternative to physical materialism was dualism, then I should have to opt for this, admittedly rather unsatisfactory, answer. It *is*, nonetheless, unsatisfactory and this encourages me to look for a better alternative to physical materialism than dualism. Happily, one is at hand in the form of 'emergence'.

Emergence

The 'emergence' theory (or family of theories) comes in two main forms. The first, 'dynamic' form suggests that the complex biological organisation of the brain gives rise to mental activity, such as thought, feeling and perception. Thus far, the theory has some similarities with physical materialism, although emergence does not imply that matter/energy is all that there is to reality. Mental activity, in turn, gives rise to 'mind', enabling humans to reflect, to make decisions, to monitor aspects of our own thinking and to have a sense of 'self'. At this point, emergence diverges significantly from physical materialism in that once mind has emerged from the brain it has, at least a limited, identity of its own, albeit one that is connected to the brain for its continued expression and, perhaps, dependent upon the brain for its continued existence. The second 'idealist' version of emergence also suggests that the brain gives rise to mental activity such as thought, feeling and perception but then diverges from dynamic emergence in proposing that this enables 'Mind', *understood in a universal sense*, to experience 'individuated' existence as 'a mind'. The individual human mind is formed through the interaction of 'Universal Mind' and a human brain/body with its attendant experiences. In this understanding of 'me', my brain and my experiences give my mind its particular *identity*, but Universal Mind gives my mind its essential *existence*. This, of course, necessitates Mind to exist either within or throughout the universe in a non-localised form that can, under certain conditions, become localised. Just as physicists think of gravity, for example, as existing throughout the universe as a 'field', but also concentrated in 'centres' (such as the Earth, the Sun or the centre of galaxies), I might consider 'Mind' to do likewise: a mental or mind-field, permeating the universe that may be manifested in and through individual brains. Human minds represent a meeting point between Universal Mind and complex brain structures and activity. This has similarities with dualism, but differs from it in that Mind is *intrinsically* part of the universe, not something that belongs to a separate category from it. Given that some physicists now postulate that the universe may contain at least fourteen dimensions (only four of which we can observe) and that our universe may be one among many, the concept of Mind existing in a universal form throughout the universe cannot be dismissed out of hand.

Strange as the thought may be, some mathematical physicists have recently proposed a theory that might give some credence to the concept of 'Mind', or something like it, permeating the universe. I have already observed that what exists at the most fundamental level of the universe in 'the quantum vacuum' is not, 'nothing'. The suggestion now, is that what lies within the quantum vacuum, is 'information' which enables matter/energy to come into existence. This 'quantum information', it is suggested, permeates the universe and undergirds its existence. This is not quite the same as saying that Universal Mind exists, but it might suggest that those who speak in such terms have touched on something that is, in fact, fundamental to the existence of the universe. I shall return to these ideas in the next chapter.

In either form of emergence (or in 'mixed' forms that take elements from both), the brain is understood as being physical, but its organisation and activity enable something 'other' that cannot be simply identified with it, to exist and this 'something other' is an individual, identifiable mind. While, as with physical materialism and dualism, there is no universally agreed mechanism by which it is understood that the physical enables the non-physical to exist in an individual, conscious form, emergence does, at least, take seriously the existence of both my brain and my mind. It also enables an understanding of human beings that retains concepts such as will, intention, reason, and, of course, consciousness. Unlike physical materialism, emergence suggests that individual minds are distinct from the physical brain processes that enable them to exist while, unlike dualism, it suggests that the brain can effectively act as an interface between matter and mind because they are intrinsically linked. It allows matter via the brain to have an effect on mind and mind via the brain to have an effect on matter.

Might Minds Exist Apart from Brains?

It is clear that human brain-mind organisation takes place at a number of levels. At a most basic level, my brain acts to regulate essential bodily functions such as breathing. At a 'higher' level it enables me to perform semi-automatic actions such as walking. These actions require a decision from me before they happen, but once the decision is made I am not normally aware of thinking about doing them. At a higher level again, I can conduct deliberate actions such as driving a car that require a level of continued concentration, even though some aspects of the activity may be semi-automatic. Higher up the scale comes concentrated thinking, perhaps about mathematics, or the meaning of life or what to eat for dinner. Finally, and most elusively, I have an ability to stand apart from all of the above activities, to be aware of them, to monitor and critique them in an experience of reflective self-awareness that gives me a sense of 'self'. I am not always aware of thinking about myself in this way and I can only do it while conscious, but it is, nonetheless, a real, if transient, ability that, almost certainly on our planet only human beings possess, and which, I suggest, enables us to achieve significant moral status.

It is possible that my mind is so dependent upon my brain's organisation and activity, that without such activity, my consciousness simply can not continue to exist. That is to say, if I were to suffer a major brain injury, the conscious aspect of my existence (my mind) might not only be 'disabled', it might be extinguished along with my damaged brain cells. There is much in our current understanding of neuroscience to suggest that this is, indeed, the case. In this version of emergence, of course, once my brain dies, my mind will die with it.

The *dynamic* form of emergence neither requires nor precludes the possibility of my mind having an ability to continue to exist apart from my brain. It may be possible in principle, for new brain cells to be developed or transplanted or for my mind to be connected to a 'resource' other than my brain and hence to continue to exist, if such a 'transfer' were possible. Odd as this might seem, some scientists working in the field of informatics, believe that eventually, technology will be perfected that will allow this to happen. Nonetheless, in the absence of such technology, *or without evidence of the existence of an alternative 'mechanism'*, I find it difficult to see how my mind could survive the dissolution of my brain. Experiments and anecdotal evidence that have been interpreted by some to indicate that individuals' minds have been able to act while 'dislocated' from their brains might suggest that the mind has some *limited* ability to extend beyond the brain, but it is not possible to go beyond this tentative conclusion. Since, in all cases of 'out of body experiences', the individuals' brains have manifestly continued to exist, it is not accurate to say that these experiences prove that minds can continue to exist apart from brains. It is, however, reasonable to suggest that these experiences *might* indicate that mental activity may be able to continue for a short period when brain activity appears to be absent.

An *idealist* version of emergence more clearly allows for the possibility of 'a mind' continuing to exist apart from the brain that gave it its individual *identity* since its *existence* is fundamentally linked, not to its brain, but to a universal mind/mental-field that has taken individuated form as a human mind. In an idealist version of emergence the onus is not so much on the need to demonstrate that individual minds *could* exist apart from brain activity (although it is unclear what they could experience if 'dislocated' from their brains), but on a need to provide *evidence* that they do. More fundamentally, there is a requirement to provide a compelling reason to believe in the existence of a universal mind/mental field in the first place.

Brain/Mind: Another Paradox?

There are aspects of my consciousness that require me to delve further into the nature of 'mind' in an attempt better to understand it and to see if there are factors that might indicate whether or not I can definitively state that my mind might be able to continue to exist apart from my brain. In thinking of them, I am reminded of my earlier road-crossing discussion. In looking at the existence of my mind and its relationship to my brain, it might be the case that personal experience and intuition, which suggest that 'I' am more than the chemical and electrical activity of my brain cells, are some way ahead of science or logic's ability to demonstrate that such is the case. This does not make my experience or intuition right, but even if a satisfactory scientific interpretation of mind is never forthcoming, it does not make them wrong.

Consciousness is a transient phenomenon. When I fall asleep my consciousness is no longer apparent to me or to anyone else. My normal *experience* of my mind is linked to my brain activity and when my brain rhythms are in a certain state, I am no longer conscious. This, of course, does not mean that my brain activity ceases completely and, there is no necessary reason to believe that my mind ceases to exist either, simply because while asleep, I am not *conscious* of its existence. If it did, 'I' would be in the very curious position of popping out of and into existence every time I fell asleep and woke up again. My conscious mind might not be evident, even to me, but there is every reason to belief that it still exists, *albeit in a latent, rather than an active form.* I cannot locate it, even if I can locate the network of neurons associated with it. I might be able to say that when these neurons are in a certain state my mind will be active, but observing their activity does not equate to observing my mind or my thoughts. Similarly, when the same neurons are in a different state I might be able to say that my mind is inactive, but it would be rash of me to conclude that my mind has, thereby, ceased to exist. I have an innate understanding that 'I' continue to exist even when I am asleep or unconscious; indeed that when 'I' wake up, I wake up as, essentially, the same person that fell asleep a few hours before. I have a sense of *continuity of being* that, while being transient and prone to periods of interruption, is something that enables me to think of me as 'me'.

My sense of self-identity and continuity of identity is, of course, *linked* to brain activity. Memories are somehow stored in my brain, or at least brain activity enables me to access them, and an ability to remember contributes much to my sense of continuity as a person. If, however, I were to awaken some morning with total amnesia, with absolutely no memory of the past, would this stop me being *essentially* the same person that went to bed quite happily the previous evening? Most certainly, I would struggle in such circumstances, but there is nothing to suggest that my personality, character, abilities and other characteristics would be utterly wiped out in such a way that I and others would accept that one person had disappeared and a new person had emerged overnight. I do not have to remember incidents from my past for them to influence what I am in the present and for them to provide a continuity link between my present and my past. In truth, if I were to add together all my conscious memories of my entire life they probably would not last longer than a few hours, but I do not doubt for an instant that all the sub-conscious memories or even memories wholly inaccessible to me influence what I now am. Similarly, when individuals awaken from long comas or when damaged neurological functions are restored, recognisably the same, if altered, persons emerge. This might indicate that the brain has a greater capacity than some suppose to create a sense of 'self', but it might equally indicate that 'self' once it has emerged has a certain identity and integrity of its own.

Experiments in the effects of drugs have indicated that some chemicals that inhibit certain brain functions also give rise to a greater sense of self-awareness, greater perception and a greater appreciation of 'reality'. While some of this may, indeed, be 'all in the mind' rather than 'in reality' it nonetheless indicates that mind is not as simply linked to brain activity as might be assumed. Such experiments have led some scientists to suggest that the brain may indeed be viewed as a *means* by which mind *interacts* with physical reality rather than being seen as the *originator* of mind which then, in turn, remains dependent upon the brain for its continued existence. Recently, neuroscientists have indicated that neural pathways in our brains are influenced by the decisions that we make with our minds. Just as it is, undoubtedly, the case that mental states are affected by brain states, it seems that brain states are also affected by mental states. For example, if I decide to practice playing the piano and then put this into effect, my mental decision and subsequent actions will create and then strengthen certain neural pathways that would not exist if I had not made such a decision in the first place. In other words, my brain is altered by the decisions that I make and by the actions that I decide to put into effect. My brain is not, in fact, simply 'hard-wired', but rather, it contains an *organic* network of connections. My brain gives rise to my mind, but is itself, refined and partly 'redrawn' by my mind. My 'refined' brain will then have an effect on my further mental processes, depending on which neural pathways and connections have been created or reinforced and on which ones have become weaker. In turn, my mind is able to make further decisions that will, again, affect the structure of my brain and so forth. It seems to me that my brain and my mind are in constant creative interaction with one another, without one being able to be reduced to the other. I am neither independent from my brain and its structure and activity nor am I wholly identified with it. This strengthens my *intuitive* belief that I exist as a moral being, able to make genuinely personal decisions.

All of this causes me to reflect that mind is an emergent feature that is as distinctive and as important, in the course of evolution as is the emergence of life from inanimate matter. How both occur may forever remain a mystery, but it is a fact that both have happened. If emergent properties can be more than just the sum of their parts it is very possible that we have only begun to understand and to explore the true emergent properties of mind. I must confess that a sense of ongoing personal identity, of 'self', is difficult to view as anything other than a mirage, and a rather cruel one at that, unless my mind, however it has emerged, has some ability to operate in its own right. I have an innate sense of being 'I' that is impossible to sustain in a physical materialist model. This does not mean that my innate sense, based perhaps more on intuition and experience than on scientifically verifiable observations, must be right, but it does, perhaps indicate, that this is an example of intuition and experience nudging me to pursue the rational arguments to their full conclusions, exploring every possibility, before I abandon any belief that 'I' exist and relinquish the totality of my personal identity to my brain cells. Such is the importance of the subject that I believe that further exploration is, indeed, justified and that it lies in the direction of examining ways in which the physical and non-physical might exist and relate beyond my personal experience of them; that is to say, at a universal level.

Chapter Four

Never Mind the Universe:
The Fundamental Nature of the Universe
(Holistic Materialism… Intrinsic Dualism… The Primacy of Mind…
Going Beyond Materialism and Dualism… The Possible
Compatibility of Theism with Reality)

Pre-cursor of Mind

So far, I have concluded that I experience both the physical and the non-physical/mental as realities in my life and that even though I cannot be certain how they interact with one another, I am convinced that they do and that somehow my brain is the focal point of that interface. While either physical materialism or dualism might be true, as explanatory theories they both create as many problems as they seek to solve. Emergence seems to be nearer the mark in helping me to understand the nature of the relationship between my brain and my mind, but there are further questions to be answered before I can embrace a form of emergence with any great degree of confidence.

When I apply these reflections to the possible relationship between the physical and the non-physical 'beyond me', what they indicate is that the universe must be of sufficient complexity to allow first, the emergence of life, and then the emergence of individual minds: two hugely significant events, by anyone's reckoning. I cannot see how this could happen unless the 'stuff' of the universe either contains *within itself* all the necessary components to make such complexity, subtlety and individuality possible or else it is *inextricably* bound to something beyond itself that makes this possible.

The existence of mind in individual human beings as well as my experience of 'self' seems to knock physical materialism on the head. There is nothing in a *purely physical* understanding of the universe that appears to be able to give rise to minds that are genuinely able to think, feel, will and intend. As I have indicated previously, physical materialism, at least in its standard form, leads inexorably to determinism and, in determinism, there is no place for freedom of thought, feeling, will or intention. If I were to insist that the theory of physical materialism is correct, I could, of course, retreat to the position that my mind does not really exist. To do so, I would have to acknowledge that all of human life is the outworking of physical processes that can, in principle, be both known and anticipated. Every thought is the end result of a physical process and is, itself, a physical thing, rendering this and other discussions literally meaningless and purposeless. There can be no meaning or purpose in a physical process; just the process itself, which is value-free. This, I believe, is an unreasonable price to pay for a theory that cannot be shown to be true; just as unreasonable as the assertion that the physical universe does not exist, but that it is the product of my mind. I think that it is, therefore, reasonable to conclude that the 'stuff' of the universe is more complex than physical materialism would allow.

One way of understanding the complexity of the universe is to propose that matter/energy either contains within it, or has 'attached' to it, a non-physical element (or elements) that I am going to term 'precursor of mind'. This is not the same as saying that there may be sub-atomic particles or forces, as yet undiscovered by physicists that might allow for the development of minds emerging from brains. Any such particles or forces would still be 'physical' and while they might help to explain the nature of ordinary matter, they would not cast any light on how matter, once it has developed into complex living organisms, might give rise to consciousness. A degree of indeterminacy may exist at a sub-atomic level, but, as I noted previously, once matter has organised itself into larger atoms and molecules, physical indeterminacy disappears; looking for more and more physical entities at a sub-atomic level does not help to explain the existence of indeterminate minds. Should it exist, this hypothetical 'precursor of mind' would have to be genuinely non-physical in order for the universe to give rise, in time, to life and, eventually, to conscious life-forms. In other words, it would not be, in itself, physical in the sense of being susceptible to being observed or measured scientifically, but it could either be intrinsic to the nature and composition of matter ('holistic materialism') or it could be inexorably bound to matter at every level of its organisation ('intrinsic dualism'). The concept of a precursor of mind is a coherent one and is worthy of some further investigation.

Beyond Materialism and Dualism

At first glance, 'holistic materialism' might seem to differ very little from physical materialism, but this impression is misleading. Physical materialism suggests that I have to accept that matter/energy simply is what it is and that, happily, it is somehow sufficiently complex and subtle to enable life and consciousness to come into existence. That is the way it is and that is all there is to say about it. Holistic materialism suggests that there is a *reason* why matter/energy is the way it is and that reason is to be found in the existence of the non-physical *within* matter/energy. I have already mentioned that some mathematical physicists are exploring the possibility that, at the most fundamental level, matter/energy emerges from 'quantum information'; something that is non-physical, but nonetheless both real and capable of giving rise to the physical universe. This, in itself, however, does not necessarily overcome my main objection to physical materialism: that everything is determined in a closed chain of cause and effect.

Quantum information might be non-physical, but once it has given rise to matter/energy there is no *essential* reason why it ought to have any further role to play in permitting indeterminate minds to emerge from the complex organisation of matter/energy in human brains. In order for holistic materialism to break free from the shackles of determinism, something *like* quantum information must lie at the heart of matter/energy, but this information must also be of such a type as to *enable* the emergence of non-physical minds. This suggests that any non-physical precursor of mind must play more that an initial creative role in establishing matter/energy; it must, itself, be of sufficient complexity and have sufficient efficacy to ensure that non-physical minds will eventually emerge. Holistic materialism is therefore, a possible way of understanding reality, but only if it is interpreted in a particular manner.

A second way of viewing the complexity of matter/energy is to suggest that it has, *bound to it*, a precursor of mind. This precursor is not physical and is linked to matter/energy in a necessary bond. This might be described as 'intrinsic dualism' in that the physical and non-physical are essentially bound together at every level. As with holistic materialism, the existence of quantum information might suggest that intrinsic dualism reflects reality, but it seems to me that this theory carries with it the inherent problems I identified earlier in classical dualism. How, it might be asked, does this non-physical precursor of mind bond with physical matter/energy and why does it do so? As with physical materialism or classical dualism, I could argue that this is simply the way it is. Alternatively, I could argue that someone or something intentionally *created* this non-physical precursor of mind and 'attached' it to matter/energy at the beginning of the universe. This might be true, but to be frank, all forms of dualism, even intrinsic dualism, seem rather clumsy and remote mechanisms for a creator to adopt. Dualism is more likely to be a creation of philosophers and theologians, determined to avoid physical materialism than it is the product of a mind capable of forming the universe. The central problem of dualism would still remain: how do the physical and the non-physical interact if they are two different types of 'stuff' or to put it in more classical language, two different substances?

It seems to me, therefore, that all forms of dualism as well as physical materialism are inadequate to explain the existence and the nature of the universe. Holistic materialism, I believe, points in a more fruitful direction, but it requires significant 'tweaking' before it escapes the problem of determinism associated with physical materialism.

The Primacy of Mind

One way of interpreting holistic materialism is to suggest that matter/energy is not simply brought into existence by quantum information, but that matter/energy is *an expression* of this information. In other words, non-physical information finds expression as matter/energy. *They are essentially one and the same*; matter/energy is a form of 'realised' information and it is this information that underlies and permeates the universe. Just what its full role and significance are, it may be impossible to say since we are not equipped to explore it other than in its realised form as matter/energy, but it is reasonable to suggest that it is of fundamental importance to everything that exists since without it, quite literally, nothing would exist.

In order for the problem of determinism to be resolved, I believe that it is possible to argue that one coherent way of understanding this fundamental information is to interpret it as Fundamental Mind. This, I know, is not the *only* way of viewing quantum information, but it seems to me to be a *valid* way of doing so. This is the essential approach taken by theology and since my goal in this part of this book is to determine if a cogent and defensible understanding of reality is compatible with belief in God, I think that it is worth exploring further.

What theology provides is an explanation for the existence of the universe that goes beyond both materialism and dualism. It proposes that the ultimate reality that lies within and behind the complexity of matter/energy is, indeed, non-physical; it is, in fact, mind in its essential and primary form. Mind gives rise to matter/energy *as an expression of itself*; it ensures that matter/energy is sufficiently complex and that physical laws and processes are sufficiently fine-tuned to enable life to arise and for individual conscious beings to exist.

It is still possible to postulate all of this in an essentially dualistic way: Mind created something other than itself (matter/energy) and it either set in motion the laws and processes necessary for matter/energy to give rise to life and individual conscious beings (deism) or it continued to interact with matter/energy, guiding its processes, enabling it to give rise to conscious beings (classical theism). Both deism and classical theism, however, suffer from the problems inherent in all dualist theories, especially the problem of how two totally different 'substances', the physical and the non-physical, can interact. There is, however, I believe a richer and more persuasive way to view the relationship between mind and matter/energy; one that can satisfy the varied requirements of philosophy, science and theology.

Rather than separating mind and matter/energy into two distinct categories, as in dualism, or suggesting that matter/energy simply gives rise to mind, as in physical materialism, I am attracted to exploring the proposition that mind is, indeed, the ultimate reality and that it manifests *itself* in, through and as matter/energy. This is a form of *idealism*, but a non-dualist form. It also shares similarities with holistic materialism, but it avoids the latter's potentially deterministic features. While this is an unusual concept to entertain, partly because of the underlying cultural assumption that some form of materialism is true, it seems to me that the idea is both coherent and plausible.

In the first instance, matter/energy may be seen, not as a different kind of 'stuff' from mind but as a specific *form* of mind. Mind and matter/energy are of the same 'stuff', just as are radio waves and electro-magnetic radiation. Just as radio waves cannot exist apart from electro-magnetic radiation, so too matter/energy cannot exist apart from mind; just as electro-magnetic radiation is greater than radio waves but encompasses them, so too, mind is greater than matter/energy but encompasses it. Just as electro-magnetic radiation is present wherever radio waves are present, but not necessarily vice-versa, so too mind is present wherever matter/energy is present but not, necessarily vice-versa.

Ultimately, in this view of reality, individual consciousness arises from matter/energy *within* the universe because matter/energy arose from mind at the *beginning* of the universe and continues to be infused and informed by it. Matter/energy without mind is a misconception since matter/energy *is a form of mind*.

A further elaboration on this understanding of mind as 'ultimate reality' is to suggest that the material universe is, in fact, a construct of a Fundamental Mind. That is to say, the universe exists *within* a Fundamental Mind which is, in fact, the sum total of reality. This is not the same as saying that the universe is imaginary; a mere thought-experiment. Such would be the case if a Fundamental Mind was either limited or was just one aspect of reality. If, however, a Fundamental Mind *is* reality, then whatever exists in a Fundamental Mind *is* real.

Just as there is no way of proving or disproving materialist or dualist theories there is, of course, no way of proving that this form of idealism is correct. It is, however, a viable philosophical and, I believe, theological proposition that can be shown not to conflict with what science has revealed about the nature of the universe. This, is a big statement and I shall have to explore it further in detail in order to see if it stands up to closer scrutiny, but it does present an alternative to both materialism and dualism. As such, it deserves my closest attention not least since these other theories have failed to impress.

Reality Check

Before continuing with this exploration I think that a reality check is now in order. I cannot escape the conviction that, in all honesty, all possible theories of how and why I have come to exist appear to me to be improbable and yet I also cannot escape the conviction that since I do exist, one of them must be true. I am prepared to accept that neither I, nor anyone else, may discover a completely correct theory, but within the confines of the broad strokes that I have been using so far, some form of idealism is, to my mind, the front-runner.

To put it differently: if matter/energy is all that there is and it just happens to be the way that it is, then I am very fortunate. Conversely, if a Fundamental Mind is ultimate reality and matter/energy is a form of mind, then… I am very fortunate. The existence of the universe and of conscious life-forms within it, are, it seems to me, incredibly unlikely occurrences, and yet, of course here I am. That I exist, at all, in a universe that contains both matter/energy and mind, is, to me, almost beyond belief, regardless of how I view the universe to have come into existence. At some point I have to admit that something simply 'was' or 'is' and that

that something is either the universe itself or something that gave rise to the universe.

Given that I have a choice between the highly improbable thought that the universe (or its antecedents) gave rise to itself in a 'physical' way and the highly improbable thought that the universe exists because of the 'primacy' of mind, there is little to choose between the options. In other words, either mind is really a form of matter/energy or matter/energy is really a form of mind. *Either might be true*, but I think that there is a greater, though unquantifiable probability, of mind rather than matter/energy enjoying primacy. I say this because I find it more coherent to think of how a primary and essential form of mind (a Fundamental Mind) could *choose* to express itself in and through a variety of forms, including physical forms, than to think of how matter/energy, without any ability to have intention, could give rise to mind as a meaningful entity that is able to think, reason, will and intend. Similarly, I find it more reasonable to perceive of mind giving rise to a universe that, in turn, gives rise to individual minds with the capacities of thought, will and intention than such minds emanating from non-volitional quantum information. *I might, of course, be wrong, but then again, I might be right.* The main issue, at this point in my enquiry, however, is not that mind *is* the ultimate reality within the universe, but that this is an entirely feasible possibility.

At this juncture, my investigation 'into God' reaches something of a watershed. So far, I have really been investigating whether or not it is sensible to think that mind exists and whether it is coherent to think of mind as being the underlying reality both within and 'behind' the universe. I have been doing so in order to test whether there is something intrinsic in the nature of the universe that precludes the existence of God and that compels me to embrace atheism. In other words, had I encountered a *convincing* argument that suggested that either physical materialism was correct or that matter/energy was *necessarily* self-existent, or that belief in mind is incoherent, my investigation could have gone no further and I should be free to embrace my natural inclination to be an atheist. In such an event, whatever my personal experiences might be or whatever my intuition might suggest, I should have to accept that they cannot be allowed to lead me to belief in God. As it is, there is ample scope to consider not only that mind exists, but that it might, indeed, be the ultimate reality behind and within the universe.

Because, this is so, I now intend to explore what this might involve and what its implications might be. I am not suggesting that, because it is *possible* that mind is the ultimate reality behind and within the universe, that such is, in fact, the case. At this point I wish simply to find out what it might mean *if* it were to be true. I am aware that what I have termed 'a Fundamental Mind', as being the ultimate reality behind and within the universe, theology might properly call, 'God'.

In other words, the first part of my enquiry suggests that belief in God is *consistent with* a coherent and defensible understanding of reality which I outlined, though this understanding of reality is not the only one that a thoughtful enquirer might come to hold.

Part Two

Can we Make Sense of God?

Chapter Five

What's in a Name? – What We Mean by 'God'

(The Concept of a Supreme Being… God as a Personal Being…
How We Talk about God… The Idea of 'Theodigms')

I have suggested in the previous chapter that 'God' is the name
that theology might give to what I called 'a Fundamental Mind':
mind in its essential and primary form. If God is viewed in this
way, theology proposes that God gave rise to the universe in such a
manner that it was enabled to give rise to individual life-forms
and, eventually, to individuals with consciousness. I suspect,
however, that this is not exactly what most people think of when
they hear or use the term 'God'; it is not even how most theologians
use the term. It is important, then, that I take some time to explore
the ways in which God can be spoken of and, in particular, to set
out ways, in which it might be appropriate for me to speak of God
before returning to a discussion of the implications of God being
'Mind'; the ultimate reality behind and within the universe.

None of this, of course, is to prejudge the issue of whether or not
God actually exists; it simply clarifies who or what it is, whose
existence or non-existence, I am trying to explore. Any time I
speak of God in this section of the book, therefore, I do so on the
understanding that I am attempting to find out what God might be
like and how God might choose to act, *should God exist*.

Like many things in life that might, at first glance, appear to be
obvious, it is not at all obvious what people mean when they speak
of 'God'. The word 'God' is precisely just that: a word.
Furthermore, it has been given a wide variety of meanings some of

which are only vaguely, if at all, related to one another. For example, the word 'God' has been used in antiquity to refer to the male super-human residents of Mount Olympus. It has been used of the impersonal 'principle' behind the Universe, to the Earth (usually in a feminine form) or to the Sun (usually in a male form). The term has been applied (in its plural form) to entities represented by various carved and sculptured statues as well as (in its singular form) to the object of devotion of the adherents of various organised religions such as Judaism, Christianity and Islam. If I were so minded, I could also use the word to refer to a pink, galaxy-eating blancmange that I consider to inhabit the outer reaches of the universe, that unfortunately has the annoying habit of disappearing every time I try to observe it, but to which I am, nonetheless, completely if somewhat irrationally, devoted.

Clearly, it is not possible to get to grips with theology unless the term 'God' is pinned down more precisely. For reasons that I outlined earlier, the God that I am exploring is 'God' as understood broadly within the context of Christianity. That is to say, it is an understanding of God that emanates from events and ideas contained within the New Testament and which is tested by philosophy, theology, science and experience, set against an appreciation of the historical background from which the New Testament emerged. This is quite a precise area of exploration (as well as quite a mouthful), although many of the arguments surrounding the nature and the existence of God are also applicable in a wider context. This means that I shall not attempt to construct a 'natural theology', arguing *solely* from reason. I have already stated that intuition and experience are important factors in enabling me to come to a decision with regard to God's existence, as well as in making decisions in a host of other areas. I also recognise that my experience and intuition offer support to the suggestion that pursuing a *Christian* understanding of God is likely to provide me with fertile territory for exploration. Nonetheless, if, in so doing, a *Christian* understanding of God appears to me to be unreasonable, then I shall look elsewhere.

In the context of Christianity (and other monotheistic religions), God is sometimes described as 'the Supreme Being who created the universe', or is referred to in some such terms. This, of course, is not a comprehensive statement about God; rather it may be seen as being the minimum statement of any real significance that can be made about God. It is, perhaps, a more specific assertion than saying that God is 'a Fundamental Mind', the ultimate reality behind and within the universe. It does not contradict this statement, but it may be seen as refining it. Of course, theology has much more to say about God than this statement provides; if this were not so, there would be little point in writing or reading this book. It is, nonetheless, a genuinely important statement for theology and it deserves proper investigation. As I have suggested, other definitions or descriptions of God are possible, but I am happy to explore this core theological description of God to see what it entails and to check if it is a coherent concept.

What's So Special About Being 'Supreme'?

In common parlance, the term 'supreme' is used rather loosely. I might use it to refer to someone I consider to be the best singer on the international stage, or to describe the best football team in a given league, or the best hotel in a tourist resort. 'Supreme' often means 'simply the best'. Of course, I have my list of supreme things; other people have theirs and they might only occasionally agree. Following this line of thought, a casual theological enquirer might conclude that if God is a Supreme Being then he, she or it is simply the best type of being that could possibly be encountered or imagined. This may, indeed, be how many people view God, and, should God exist, it might also be true, but this is not quite what the term 'supreme' means when employed in the context of theology.

By 'supreme,' theologians usually mean, not that God is the biggest or the best, but that God is in a class of God's own: God is totally unique. God is not one part of the universe, albeit a very big and important part. In the context of understanding God as a Fundamental Mind, this suggests that mind is not merely a component part of the universe to be set alongside other features such as gravity and electro-magnetism, but is, rather, its primary, under-girding feature. Being unique, God could, in principle, exist apart from the universe that we inhabit, even if, as I wish to suggest, God has chosen not to do so. The universe, however, could not exist apart from God.

This does not mean that God is unable to relate to the universe. Classical theism has always held that God is able to relate to the universe and to creatures within it, although it is not altogether clear how this can happen if God and the universe are set in absolute contrast to one another in a dualist sense, as is often the case. If, however, God is understood as a Fundamental Mind and, as suggested in the last chapter, matter/energy is a *form* of mind, then a non-classical form of theism might suggest that the universe is an *expression* of God, albeit a partial expression. As such, God might have chosen not to express God-self in this way or God could have chosen a very different kind of universe as a means of self-expression. To use philosophical language, the universe is *contingent*, dependent upon God for existence, whereas God is *necessary*, having existence within God-self. This is the fundamental distinction between God and everything else; not a distinction of what type of 'stuff' God and the universe are (as in many expressions of classical theism), but a distinction of *being*. This understanding of the relationship between God and the universe, I am going to term, *dynamic theism* as it places the emphasis on God acting to produce the universe as a means of self-expression rather than on God and the universe belonging *essentially* to two separate realms of existence.

Classical theism cannot be discounted as a viable philosophical and theological theory and it has many supporters. They might even suggest that what I am describing as dynamic theism is, in fact, a version of classical theism. Nonetheless, it seems to me that what I have termed dynamic theism holds the best prospect for providing me with a theology that is in keeping with my understanding of reality and with the insights of science, so, for the most part, my continued examination of what I mean by 'God' will pursue dynamic, rather than classical, theism as generally understood. Classical theism will, no doubt, continue to have no shortage of proponents.

It is difficult to find appropriate language to describe the essential relationship between God and the universe that does not imply either that they are two utterly distinct things (a form of dualism) or that God and the universe are simply two ways of describing the one thing (pantheism). I am aware that other writers have chosen a variety of terms to distinguish God from the universe (avoiding pantheism) without making them wholly separate twin-aspects of reality (thereby, avoiding dualism). To a degree, the choice of words is somewhat arbitrary, but in pursuit of dynamic theism, I am going to use two widely accepted terms, though not necessarily in quite the same way as some theologians might utilise them. I am going to employ the word 'transcendent' to describe God's *distinction* from the universe and the word, 'immanent' to describe God's *unity* with the universe. By 'transcendent' I mean that God is a 'first-order' being while all other things are derivative from God and by 'immanent' I mean that the universe cannot be separated from God at any level of its existence. From time to time, I shall also use the rather less technical terms, 'apart from' to refer to transcendence and, 'in' to refer to immanence.

In order to be supreme, it is reasonable to infer that God is totally independent and self-sufficient, reliant on no one and on nothing else for anything. God is the original and *only* self-made being. By definition, (should God exist) God does not rely on anyone or anything else for existence, for purpose, for meaning, for relationship or for anything at all. Being transcendent, I do not expect that God's existence can be scientifically verified, utilising tools that are limited to verifying things that lie wholly within the universe; how *could* such be the case? If God is also immanent I do not, however, expect that God's existence will be falsified by scientific enquiry. If science or anything else were to 'prove' God's existence, then, it seems to me, that God could be contained within the universe and would not be supreme. For that reason, instead of being dismayed that there is no 'proof' of God's existence, I am quite content that such is the case. If, however, science, or anything else, were to 'prove' that God *could not* be immanent 'in' the universe, (even though, in principle, God could still exist *apart* from the universe), I should have to conclude that all talk of God is meaningless since, even if God did exist, the fact is of no relevance to me. *In essence, I suspect that if God does exist and if God is both transcendent and immanent then I ought to find that such theological reflections are compatible with science though not verifiable by it.*

By saying that God is supreme, I also understand theology to be saying that God is not simply one of a number of transcendent beings or even that God is the biggest and best of such beings. If God is 'supreme', then should such 'extra-universal' beings exist, they too are created by God and God is as unique in comparison to them as God is to beings within the universe. Ultimately and definitively, God is supreme. '*God is in a category of one*' might not be a very catchy slogan, but it may be the closest that theologians will ever get to finding one that 'describes' God.

I suggest that it is reasonable to believe that *if* God exists and is a Supreme Being, then God is *totally* self-sufficient. I take this to mean that God does not need the existence of anyone or anything else to 'add' something *definitively new and positive* to God's experience of existence. This is an important point since, at a popular level at least, some forms of classical theism may be understood to suggest that by creating the universe, God has, in fact, added something to God's own existence. If, for example, the existence of human beings, or other creatures, gives God an *extrinsic* experience of relationship that God did not otherwise have, then God has 'added' something definitively new to God-self. If, however, God experiences relationship *intrinsically*, creation at most adds 'more of the same' or 'more of a lesser version of the same'. It is a challenge, therefore, to view 'simple monotheism' as indicating that God is a Supreme Being, although God may still be seen as being a unique, original and very powerful being. That, of course, would be significant, but not as significant as being 'supreme'.

Is God a Person?

The answer to this question is not, I fear, as straight forward as many people might wish or claim; the answer is, in fact, 'yes' *and* 'no'. It is 'yes' in so far as God's existing, being self-aware, thinking, willing and relating are concerned. As a Supreme Being, God is not an inanimate object, nor is God an impersonal set of rules such as the 'laws' of mathematics or physics. In that sense, clearly, God is a person. 'Mind' requires thought and that is a faculty that I associate with personal beings.

In a more fundamental sense, however, God is not a person; rather God is 'above and beyond' being a person. My understanding of 'person' is essentially a human one; it cannot really be otherwise. In truth I have a difficult job trying to define what a human person is, never mind trying to define what a divine person is. I might even wonder if some animals are 'persons', although not quite persons in the same sense as humans. If I say that a person is a being that has, or may have, the ability to think, to have purpose, to be self aware and to relate, then humans, God and arguably some animals are persons. If, however, I say that these various faculties and abilities, if they could be exhaustively understood, *define* who or what a person is and that this *definition* can be applied to God, then clearly I am not doing justice to God as a Supreme Being if I were to say that God is a person. I cannot, at one and the same time, say that God is transcendent and then attempt to *define* God using terms drawn from human experiences which occur entirely within the universe.

There are many things about God as a person that cannot properly be said or even known. God cannot be understood as being either male or female; hence the consistent use of the word 'God' throughout this book, rather than 'he' or 'she', even though, at times, this may make for rather stilted prose. If God were either male or female then God could not be supreme. If, for example, God were male, then God would be 'missing' positive female qualities, attributes and experiences. A Supreme Being, may be more than 'simply the best', but, of course, a Supreme Being cannot be 'less than the best'. God cannot lack positive attributes that other beings possess and so, cannot be thought of as being either male or female. At the same time, since God cannot be less than either male or female. God must combine positively all that we associate with gender, while surpassing it.

Similarly, God cannot be located spatially. I cannot say God is 'here' but not there'. If such were the case, then God would again, be 'missing' something by being in only one place at a time. Something that was in a place where God was not, would have experiences and perceptions that were not available to God, undermining the concept of God being supreme. In the same vein, God cannot be present 'now' but not also present 'then', whether 'then' refers to the past or the future. If, as some physicists indicate, time is not really a linear procession of past, present and future events, but is a dimension that simply 'is', then if God is supreme, God must be in all of time… all of the time. Finally, if God is a Supreme Being, God cannot lack any kind of knowledge for if such were the case God would, in fact, be missing quite a lot and, hence, could not be supreme.

I do need to introduce one important caveat at this point: when I speak of God 'not missing' anything, I am referring to positive attributes and experiences. I cannot see that God is 'missing' anything by not having negative experiences (such as non-existence). It seems to me that for the term to be meaningful, the concept of being supreme implies perfection rather than having a plethora of imperfections. I know that I cannot logically prove that this ought to be so, but I have already said that I am exploring whether or not a *Christian* understanding of God is reasonable; I am not exploring a purely philosophical concept. Thus, experiences of God disagreeing with God-self or God rebelling against God's will or God being weak are not *necessary* for a Supreme Being to be supreme.

So, what sort of 'person' is God? It seems to me that I can give two answers to this question. I could say that God, as a Supreme Being, is 'personal' but is not a 'person' as we humans know it. Conversely, I could state that God is the one and only true 'person' that exists and that human beings are 'personal beings', but not true persons. Either way, the distinction between God and other beings is maintained.

Can We Really Say Anything About God at All?

The thoughts expressed so far in this chapter (or thoughts similar to them) have prompted some people to throw their hands in the air and to exclaim that there is no point in trying to talk about a

Supreme Being at all since, by definition such a being is essentially incomprehensible. How can we possibly say anything about a being that is so definitively in a category of its own? This is a serious issue (though, perhaps more so for an advocate of classical theism than for someone who wishes to explore dynamic theism) and is one that needs to be tackled head on.

First the bad news: at a very fundamental level, God *is* incomprehensible. Anyone who is transcendent, who is not contained within the universe must, at least *in part*, be incomprehensible to anyone inside the universe. Indeed, the 'part' of God that is incomprehensible to humans is God's essential being. Those living inside the universe know nothing of what existence 'apart from' the universe is like. 'What is it like 'apart from' the universe?' is like asking 'what does a colour that no one has ever seen look like?' If I were to imagine that I suddenly had the ability to see a hitherto unseen colour lying somewhere in the infra-red range of the electro-magnetic spectrum, how could I possibly go about describing it to someone else?

Such a task may be impossible to complete fully, but a number of approaches come to mind that might help me convey at least a sense of what this colour is. In the first instance, in trying to describe this new colour to others I might begin by saying what the colour is like (that is, if it *is* like another colour that I can identify). So, I might say that it is 'like' bright yellow and at the same time that it is 'like' bright red. This would not describe the new colour but it would help to give some sort of reference point for it: it is a bright colour, likely to have a stimulating effect on the senses and it is likely to be eye-catching, if only other eyes were able to catch it. This approach is sometimes called *description by analogy*.

Secondly, I might say what this colour is *not* like. I could say that it is definitely not like an insipid grey. This, again, would not describe the new colour but it would help others to get some understanding of it. Presumably, it is *not* a colour that would have a depressing effect (or calming effect if that is how some people view grey) or a colour that could be easily ignored. This approach is sometimes called *description by negation*. If I were to put together information about what the colour is like and what the colour is not like (analogy and negation), some sort of appreciation of the new colour may begin to form in the minds of those who have not seen it. Even so, they would still not be able to see the actual colour.

This illustration is, of course, an imperfect one, but with its limitations acknowledged, I can apply it to my knowledge of God. I may meaningfully discuss what God is like and what God is not like and in so doing build up a meaningful, if rather limited, picture of God within the confines of my human understanding. For example, I might say that God is like a kind and loving father or mother but that God is not like a spiteful and uncaring Landlord. Of course, I may be right or wrong in what I am saying, and just how I and others may judge whether or not I am talking nonsense, I shall discuss later. In principle, however, I can use the methods of analogy and of negation to enable me to talk about God as a Supreme Being.

This approach, though, will not take me very far; there is only so much than one can say by way of analogy or negation before grinding to a halt. There is a third way, however, in which talk about God can be meaningful and that is by *approximation*. If I acknowledge that I cannot talk definitively about God, I can still contend that I can talk in a limited, yet correct, way about God.

One of the first chemistry lessons that I attended at school taught me to recognise and to understand a simple diagram of the atom. This diagram consisted of a circle with one or more points orbiting it and was, I believe, called a Bohr diagram. This, I was told, is what an atom looks like. As I progressed in my studies (though not very far in chemistry) the simple Bohr diagram became ever more complex. Had I studied chemistry or physics at university the Bohr diagram would have transformed itself into ever more complicated explanations of the atom until eventually, I would have been confronted by a page covered in formulae and equations.

These complicated images are more accurate and contain more information than the earlier simpler diagrams but they too are only approximations to the real thing: *they are not actual atoms*. At the same time, the earlier approximations are not wrong; *they are simply limited*. In this way, as long as I recognise that all of my talk about God is approximate, I can talk meaningfully within recognised limitations, and that, it seems to me, is what much of theology, *as distinct from dogma*, is about.

This is, I believe, a very important point. The very best that I or anyone else can ever attain, is an approximate understanding of God. I may discover or even promote a model that describes God in part, but I will never find a model that describes God exhaustively, never mind one that truly defines God. This statement has enormous implications for everything that philosophers and theologians have ever said about God. If I understand all theology, including theology within religions other than Christianity, to provide me with approximate statements that *might* point towards the reality of God (if God exists) rather than with comprehensive statements that seek to *define* God, I am able both to recognise their limitations and also to be encouraged to seek further illumination. Of course, few, if any, theologies are perfectly accurate even within their limitations, but in so far as they are accurate they present me with *pointers* to God. Instead of viewing them as being *necessarily* in competition with one another, I may view them as being, *to some degree*, complementary, even if this is not always how their proponents view them. Some may be readily understood as being simpler than others, while others may be of similar complexity but emphasise different aspects of God or come to the topic from different perspectives, but might still be valid 'God-pointers'. Exercising my limited knowledge of Greek I am going to coin a new word and term all such approximations, *theodigms*.

Such *theodigms* might only give me partial 'access' to God, but that ought to be seen as a strength rather than a weakness as it is quite impossible for me to understand God as God really 'is'. Even if I were somehow able to come close to a full intellectual understanding of God, however, this would not, in and of itself, enable me to *relate* to God; it is very difficult to relate to a concept, however refined it might be. Equally, I may be able to relate to God intuitively, without much intellectual understanding at all. Nonetheless, *if God exists*, I feel that I need a meaningful *theodigm* through which I might understand something about God; something that gives some 'content' to a Supreme Being with whom I believe I may have a relationship. Without such a *theodigm*, I fear that both my theology and my spirituality will descend into an amorphous void.

Viewing theology as presenting me with various *theodigms* also suggests that when I and others either accept or reject a particular understanding of God it is not necessarily God that we are accepting or rejecting, but a *theodigm*. *Theodigms* may provide access to God, but they are not God. I suspect that it is often the case that individuals settle on a *theodigm* that they are comfortable either to accept or to reject because that is as far in their theological enquiry as they feel they need to go. For both theists and atheists, there is always 'further to go'; more *theodigms* to explore. That, to my mind, is part of what makes theology and God (should God exist) so fascinating.

Finally, there is another way in which talk about God and knowledge of God can be meaningful. This is not so much a fourth way, but rather a way that helps the other three ways have real 'content'. God, as God exists in and of God-self, is fully accessible only to God. God, however, may choose to reveal to humans (or others) as much of God-self as God desires and I think that it is reasonable to suggest that God would do so. Just how much of God, God might choose to reveal at any given time or place, will depend on a number of factors that I shall explore later, but to anticipate some of that discussion, I think that it is reasonable to expect that 'revelation' will be both partial and progressive. This suggests that it is *essential* to embrace the idea of *theodigms* as being integral to theology. If revelation occurs, and if it is both partial and progressive as well as being partially and progressively appreciated and understood, then *theodigms* ought to be continually refined in the light of ongoing revelation and reflection. Nonetheless, this does not alter the basic proposition that if the universe is an expression of God, consisting of the same 'stuff' as God, then revelation is possible. Indeed, if the universe is an expression of God, then it might be argued that some degree of revelation is inevitable.

That God might reveal part of God-self to humans while being known fully only to God-self is not so very different from what I and others do in our own lives all the time. While, unlike God, I may not know myself completely, I certainly have a more intimate knowledge of myself than anyone else. Nonetheless, I reveal either intentionally or unintentionally, aspects of my character, personality and thoughts to others. The 'real me', is known only to me and to God (should God exist) while the 'revealed me' is accessible to others. Of course, the 'revealed me' may be deliberately falsified if I wish to cover up some of my less attractive characteristics, but by and large, the 'revealed me' and the 'real me' will overlap considerably because, essentially they refer to the same person.

In a similar fashion, the 'real' God and the 'revealed God' overlap. Since God is a Supreme Being with nothing to hide from others, neither needing nor desiring approval or commendation and not fearing disapproval or condemnation, there is no reason for God to reveal anything other than what is really there. So, even though I can never know God as God knows God, I can know God as God reveals God-self to me, within the limitations of human aptitude. Human understanding of God's revelation will never quite capture all that has been revealed; hence, as stated above, the requirement to take seriously the concept of *theodigms*. Just what God is like or not like, just what form my *theodigms* may take and just what it is that God has revealed of God-self, will exercise my mind for the next few chapters.

Chapter Six

To Be or Not To Be: God and the Existence of the Universe

(Who Made God?... Time and Space... The Nature of Matter)

When I spoke in the previous chapter of God as 'the Supreme Being who created the universe', I mentioned that God (should God exist) is transcendent in relation to the universe but also that God is immanent and hence, able to relate to it. I now want to pursue the thought of immanence further.

If God were not immanent we would have two separate types of things each 'supreme' in its own sphere: God in 'God's world' and the universe in... well, the universe. Of course, this state of affairs would negate the whole idea of God being a Supreme Being since, as I have already argued, 'supreme' does not mean biggest or best, but rather 'one and only'. If God is the 'one and only' then the universe (or perhaps 'multi-verse' as some cosmologists postulate), must have been created by God. It is not possible to say that God is a Supreme Being if some other entity has existence within itself, existing in its own right, apart from God. If this was so, then God would indeed, be missing something; in this case a whole universe! By any account such a gap is sizeable and any Supreme Being shuffling around in its own 'world' either unaware of the universe or existing in parallel with it does not seem very supreme to me. Even if I were to argue that God is able to gain some sort of second-hand knowledge of the universe, this would still diminish God and a Supreme Being that is diminished is no longer a Supreme Being.

When philosophers and theologians say that God is a Supreme

Being, they usually include in this concept the idea that God alone has existence within God-self and that all other things owe their existence to God. I take it that this is what is signified by belief in creation: not any particular theory about *how* God brings other things into existence, but the assertion that God has brought, and will bring, all other existing things into existence. God is the only self-existent being or thing that exists and God chose freely to create the universe. That the creation of *any particular universe* is a free choice, is a corollary of God being a Supreme Being since a Supreme Being cannot be caused to act in a particular way by anything other than itself. The *activity* of creation, however, may be viewed as the outworking of an *intrinsic* aspect of God's nature: creativity. As such, it is an *inevitable* consequence of God's existence. I shall return later to this idea, to examine some of its far-reaching implications.

So, Who Made God?

This question is probably as old as the first human who came to believe that there might be a Supreme Being, responsible for creating the earth (however he or she may have understood 'the earth'). How the idea of a Supreme Being first presented itself to human beings and then came to dominate human discussion about 'ultimate things' ever since is, itself, a fascinating issue, and I shall look briefly at that later. Nevertheless, hot on the heels of the idea that a Supreme Being (God) might exist must have come the question, 'who made God?' This is often the first really theological question that children ask as they grapple with the idea of God, inevitably thinking of God as a bigger version of 'us'; in truth, this question may be the only really theological question that some people ever ask. From time to time, the question is produced as a sort of trump card at the end of a conversation on creation and evolution with the implication that the unanswerable question has just been asked and the hapless theist must now shift uncomfortably, look down at his or her feet and mumble, 'I don't know'.

This is unfortunate as it appears to emanate from a persistent inability to see God as anything other than a bigger version of us. It seems to me that both theists and atheists are constantly susceptible to this type of thinking. Casual terms of endearment such as 'the Man upstairs' or derogatory terms such as 'the Policeman in the sky', indicate that theists and atheists alike are prone to unintentional anthropomorphism.

The *essential* concept of God is that God is self-existent: God owes nothing to anyone or to anything else. God is totally and completely self-sufficient. Asking the question, 'who made God?' is like asking, 'why are bachelors unmarried men?' A bachelor is an unmarried man because by definition that is what a bachelor is. No one or no thing made God because, by definition, God is self-existent. Any answer, other than this, falls into the trap of failing to see and to understand God as a Supreme Being; we are then back to viewing God simply as the biggest and the best version of us.

It is important to point out that describing God as a self-existent being does not imply that God *actually* exists anymore than asserting that all bachelors actually exist; there are, after all, many examples of bachelors in fiction as well as in reality. The point is not that this description of God 'proves' God's existence (contrary to the famed ontological proof of the existence of God), but that part of what I am seeking to discover when I ask if God exists, is whether or not belief in a 'self-existent' being is reasonable. Of course it may be argued that the idea of a self-existent being or thing is incomprehensible; everything, surely, has to come from something else. This may appear to be true at the 'common sense' level of my everyday experiences but, as I indicated earlier, this cannot be the case when I think of the ultimate origin of everything.

If for the moment, I remove God from the scene, I am still left with a universe to explain. As I have already discussed, I can do this by saying that the universe itself simply 'is': *it* is self-existent. A further possibility is that I can push back the existence of something that is self-existent by saying that the universe had a beginning, as scientists believe in the 'Big Bang', and that *something else, already existent* gave rise to this. Perhaps some inherently creative entity contained within itself what we call the 'laws of mathematics' or the 'laws of physics' and gave rise to the universe. Perhaps these 'laws' are, themselves somehow inherently creative, have always existed and gave rise to the universe.

I might also argue that our universe has been eternally expanding and contracting, or, perhaps, that it is part of an indeterminate series of universes. Any one of these explanations may, indeed, be correct, but none of them addresses the issue of who or what made the universe or universes or the laws of mathematics or physics, unless I am prepared to grant to at least one of these things the attribute of having existence within itself. 'The universe just is' provides no escape from the requirement to attribute self-existence to *something*. For theists to say that God is self existent does not, of course, prove that God exists but there ought to be no difficulty in accepting the cogency of the statement that self-existence is an integral 'aspect' of God, *should God exist*. Someone or something has to have its existence within itself for the universe to exist, whether that someone or something is God, the universe itself or some other unknown entity.

'In the Beginning... '

In a vain attempt not to be predictable, I tried very hard not to use this biblical phrase, but I simply cannot think of a better way of introducing the idea that the concept of creation necessarily carries within it the idea that the universe that I am part of did not always exist. To be more precise, it carries within it the idea that the universe had a beginning. That beginning was a beginning of everything that I can identify from the 'laws' of physics, known to me entirely from within the universe itself. As far as I am aware, this includes time, so I cannot really speak of the universe once not existing. There was no 'before' the universe began, since time (at least as I can know it) came into existence with the universe. Rather, as far as theology is concerned, there *is* the universe which had a beginning and there *is* God who had no beginning. Time exists within the universe but time does not exist as an *intrinsic* aspect of God.

Space and time are two aspects, perhaps the defining aspects, of one thing: the universe. They are the ways in which we map things and events within the universe; they are what scientists call 'dimensions'. There are almost certainly other dimensions within the universe; just how many is a matter of discussion among physicists and cosmologists, a discussion so complicated that it makes anything that theology can come up with appear elementary. Since, by definition, time and space are dimensions within the universe, I cannot speak of them existing 'prior to', or 'outside of' the universe. There is no time and there is no place 'outside' the universe or if there is, I can say nothing about them since my understanding of both time and space is intrinsically linked with, and limited to, my understanding of them within the universe. Even if I were to postulate that our universe is part of a series of universes, I still cannot speak of time 'before' the universe since my concept of time is entirely dependent upon my experience of this universe. Perhaps 'time' could exist before the universe and perhaps 'space' could exist outside the universe but both of these would be totally unknowable to me, so unknowable that I should really have to call them something else.

This means that as far as God's *essential* 'life' is concerned, God is both timeless and 'space-less'. 'Apart from' the universe, God cannot be said to be 'here' or 'there' as 'apart from' the universe there is no 'here' or 'there'. Similarly, 'apart from' the universe, God cannot be said to exist 'then' or 'now' since 'apart from' the universe there is no 'then' or 'now'. I cannot meaningfully talk of anything or anyone existing 'before' the universe and I cannot meaningfully talk of anything or anyone existing 'outside' of the universe (even though, of course, this is how we often speak). Space and time, as I know them, began with the creation of the universe and the terms have no meaning 'apart from' the universe.

It might reasonably be asked, what sort of existence is timeless and space-less? The answer is that, as a creature that lives my life within the boundaries of time and space, I simply can never know. The concept is, I believe, coherent, but any insight into what it is actually like is impossible. I am back to trying to explain the colour that no-one else can see. The only answer that I can give is that a timeless and space-less existence is the sort of existence that God has. Following on from the earlier discussion on how I may speak meaningfully of the unknowable, I can say, however, by way of analogy and approximation, that such an existence is like living in an 'eternal present' in which everything that from my perspective has ever happened, is happening and will ever happen, is experienced simultaneously, in one instant. Such talk is, of course, approximate and analogous as I am still using 'time' terminology to describe something that is timeless, but it may help in gaining some understanding of God's experience. Similarly, using the language of analogy and approximation, a 'space-less' existence may be viewed as God being 'everywhere'.

If I were to imagine space-time being represented by an ever-expanding balloon, one that had no limitations to its expansion, then my perspective would be that of a single point on the surface of the balloon. God's essential perspective would be that of the entire balloon. For me, there would be a past and a future; a here and a there. For God there would be an 'is' and an 'everywhere'

All of this might make God appear to be somewhat remote and disengaged from the universe and if this were all that could be said on the matter, such would be the case. Happily, however, much more can and ought to be said about God as a Supreme Being, creating the universe.

Implicit in the concept of creation is the idea that, among other things, God brought into existence space and time. As Supreme Being, God cannot be 'missing' anything and this must include experiences that lie within God's creation. This is not to say that God must experience everything in the sense that God must 'be' a star, an atom, an earthworm or anything else that exists in the universe, but it must surely mean that God has true and full knowledge of all of creation. Everything that exists in the universe must be utterly and comprehensively known to God. God does not have to be an earthworm, but God must have complete and utter knowledge of the existence and the experience of every earthworm. Jesus put it rather more poetically when he said that not a single sparrow falls to the ground without God's knowledge; not a single hair on our heads goes unnumbered by God. If this were not the case, then God would be 'missing' something; something would be outside God's knowledge and experience and if this were so, then God could not be a Supreme Being.

This does not mean, however, that God must be so identified with the universe that the universe *is*, in some sense, God (pantheism.) It does mean, though, that every single piece of creation as well as the sum of all of its parts is utterly, totally and completely known by God. God is 'in' every part of it and experiencing every part of it, not merely as an 'external' observer but also as a personal Being who not only created the universe but who also undergirds and *infuses* its continued existence. God's participation in the universe extends beyond merely 'setting it up' (Deism). It also extends to God actively and intimately sustaining the existence of the universe and everything in it.

To return to the balloon illustration, God's perspective is not only that of the entire balloon, it is also that of every point (an infinite number) on the balloon. God is both transcendent and so, 'beyond' space and time and God is 'in' the universe and so experiences space and time. As long as matter/energy is viewed as being an aspect of mind and the universe as a creative expression of God, I cannot see that there is any real difficulty in viewing God in this way. For classical theism, with its essential *ontological* separation of God from the universe, I think that greater (though not insurmountable) problems exist; a further indication, perhaps that dynamic theism is likely to provide a better way of understanding God's relationship with creation.

What's the Matter?

In suggesting that, at the most fundamental level, matter/energy has emerged from mind in the form of the universe emerging from God through a deliberate choice of God, I am stating that God and the universe are made of the same 'stuff'. The set of theories that suggests that everything that exists is, essentially, made from the same 'stuff' is called monism and, unless I embrace dualism, some form of monism is inescapable. Either, matter/energy and mind are essentially the same or else they belong to two different categories. If they belong to two distinct categories, then I have to take it on trust that either they exist in separate, but overlapping worlds or else, in some way that seems to be beyond explanation, one gave rise to the other. Understanding how two distinct categories can interact in this way is a real obstacle in the path of accepting dualism and I am prepared, therefore, to view monism as being more likely to provide insight into the nature of the universe.

To borrow mathematical language, mind and matter/energy describe everything within the universe with one being the universal set and the other being a sub-set within it. Either matter/energy is the essential form of reality (the universal set) and gave rise to mind (the sub-set) or else, mind is the essential form of reality and gave rise to matter/energy. In principle, either could be correct, but, given my experience of both mind and matter/energy, I find it more persuasive to see how mind could express itself as matter/energy, than the other way round. I have, therefore, suggested that essentially, God is mind (others might say 'Spirit', to use language employed in the Christian and other Scriptures) and that matter/energy is a form of mind, albeit, at certain levels of organisation, a rather 'physical' form.

To move from mathematics to chemistry to provide an imperfect illustration, I might suggest that just as the compound H_2O can exist in the very different forms of gas, liquid and solid, each with different characteristics, so too, theology suggests, mind can be thought of as existing as 'pure' mind (Spirit) or as sub-atomic energy/particles or as evidently physical matter/energy that characterises what we see and touch in the observable universe. Mind also exists in the forms of dark energy and dark matter and, perhaps, in a whole variety of forms as yet unthought-of by scientists, philosophers and theologians alike. All of this follows from the statement that mind (God) is the fundamental reality that underlies and undergirds the universe and that mind (God) has chosen, *in part*, to express itself in and as the universe and everything contained within it. It is worth pointing out that this last sentence does not concur with the commonly expressed belief that God made the universe 'out of nothing' and it is of monumental significance. Consequently, I shall explore it more fully in the next chapter, but first I wish to indicate another important corollary of the universe being composed of the same 'stuff' as God.

Theology suggests that the reason matter/energy is as complex as it is and why it manifests the qualities that it does, is that, fundamentally, it mirrors God. *If true*, this provides an indication why we, rightly, view nature as being something that is intrinsically important. In art, literature and in the care of the environment, human beings have always demonstrated an innate appreciation of the intrinsic value of nature that goes beyond its instrumental usefulness to our species. Again, this does not prove that God exists and that the universe is an expression of God, but it does indicate that such a belief is in keeping with some of the human race's deepest instincts.

This view of the relationship between God and the universe helps me to understand not only why matter/energy is so complex and so downright fascinating, but it also helps me to see why it is 'information-bearing'. All matter contains within it 'information' (encoded by humans as formulae utilised in physics, chemistry and biology) that not only defines itself but which in combination with other matter enables increasingly complex atoms and molecules to emerge which in turn enables 'life' to be generated and reproduced. Ultimately, it enables us as human beings with our minds, our emotions, our relationships, with our 'selves', to exist within the universe. At one level, mind may be seen as being all about information and communication, with God enjoying absolute and complete knowledge (information) and relationship (communication). If true, this understanding of reality has huge implications for an understanding of human dignity and destiny, but, at present I simply wish to suggest that it enables us to see the universe as a great and complex creation of God that exists in order to bring into existence, beings with whom God may relate.

Viewing mind and matter/energy as different expressions of the same 'stuff' also enables me to see how it is possible to speak of human life *perhaps* having the potential to continue to exist, in some form, after physical death. This is an important topic in theology and one that I shall address more fully later, but it is worth mentioning briefly at this point. Emergence suggests that my mind has been made possible through the physical organisation of my brain because the matter that makes up my brain is, itself, an expression of mind. It is, therefore, possible that *my* mind might continue to exist after my brain ceases to function if it is, in some way, taken into or sustained by mind in the 'form' of God. If God, as 'mind', has created the universe and continues to sustain it, then it seems entirely plausible that God might choose to continue to sustain the minds that have emerged within the universe after their brains have expired. Again, it is important to point out that I am not saying that such is *necessarily* the case; merely that it is *possible* given the understanding of reality and of God that I have been outlining.

Before looking more closely at the implications of all of this for a theology of creation, I want also to suggest that there is, of course, no essential reason why human beings ought to be the only creatures with minds in the universe, even though it is unlikely that we shall see any of them alighting from flying saucers or abducting people from deserted country roads in the middle of the night. Similarly, there is no obvious reason why 'our' universe ought to be the only one that exists. As I wish to explore in the next chapter, a Supreme Being is likely to be *supremely* creative, so I ought to expect a vast, indeed an infinite, array of creative expressions of God to exist.

Chapter Seven

Why Bother? – God and Creation
(Evolution… God, Humans and Freewill)

Creation and Evolution

I intend to say very little about the creationist-evolutionist debate. The truth is that, in spite of volumes having been written on the topic, it seems to me that there is very little of real significance to say about it from a theological perspective. It is *possible* that if God so wanted, God could have created the universe a few thousand years ago by divine command and then set in motion certain laws to make the universe work. God might also have created the whole thing in such a way that it appears to the enquiring mind that the universe is about fifteen billion years old, thus requiring faith to attribute its existence to God. Such *could* be the case, and creationism (a recent 'development' in the history of theology) asserts that something like this is, indeed, the truth. There is, however, no valid reason for insisting that this is so; an appeal to a particular interpretation of the opening chapters of Genesis is certainly insufficient to command adherence to this theory.

It is *also possible* that God devised an impersonal set of universal laws, enabling the universe as we know it to exist and to flourish, utilising such processes as probability and natural selection. Again, such might be the case and there are no radical implications for belief in the *existence* of God if such a theory is correct. Once again, however, there is nothing to indicate that this must be the truth and much, I think, to be said against God choosing to act in such an impersonal way. There is nothing in evolutionary theory, however, that demonstrates that the processes of probability and natural selection are such that they preclude God utilising them even if, as I wish to suggest, God is likely not to have acted in quite such a remote manner.

To be clear then, I am saying that either 'classical' creationism or 'classical' evolution *could* be true and while both of these might cause me to wonder why God would choose to act in such ways, there is nothing in either of them to call into question the existence of God and there is nothing in either of them that can absolutely disprove the other. Just as classical theism might be correct and dynamic theism wrong in spite of its attractiveness, *either* classical creationism or classical evolution might be correct. I suspect strongly, however, that neither of them is.

Classical creationism is not only irreconcilably contrary to scientific consensus, which includes the opinions of leading theistic scientists, but it suggests that God is acting out something of a charade, creating the universe in one way, but making it look as if it came into existence in another manner. While I am prepared to accept that, in theory, there could be valid reasons for God so acting, I cannot think of any compelling reasons to support this assertion. In the absence of such compelling arguments I can see no reason to go against the grain of scientific consensus.

Classical evolution, with its emphasis on the inexorable playing out of impersonal forces, 'guided' by mathematical laws that are ultimately worked out purely through chance and natural selection, strikes me as making God something of a cross between a disenchanted inventor and an absent care-taker. The problem with classical evolution is not that God could not have used such a process; it is, rather, that it suggests that God is not personally involved in God's creation; again, a rather odd way for a Supreme Being to act.

If what I have been exploring in dynamic theism is correct: that the universe has emerged from God because God is *inherently* creative and has given rise to the universe (or multi-verse) by choosing to express God-self in this way, then the universe is *intrinsically* united with God and God is subsequently united with the universe. To lapse into the analogical use of time-language, 'once' God created the universe, while it and God may still be viewed as being *logically* distinct, the universe is not *empirically* distinct from God. Since, in dynamic theism, the universe is a creative expression of God and is suffused at every level and in every way by God, it is no longer possible *experientially*, to separate the universe from God. Whatever happens within the universe, God experiences; nothing is 'missed' by God. Similarly, God's 'character' suffuses the universe in such a way that whatever God 'is', this is reflected in the universe. It cannot be the case that the universe or anything within it is essentially separate from or contrary to God as far as its existence is concerned. As I shall explore later, this does not mean that sentient beings within the universe may not exercise, at least to a limited degree, 'free-will', including an exercise of will that opposes God's character, but their existence and their ability to so act, is bound entirely to God's presence 'within' them. This is a thought of enormous significance, but for the moment, I want first, to explore the importance of the ontological link between God and the universe.

What's the Point?

If, instead of God either metaphorically snapping God's fingers and creating the universe as an extrinsic 'thing', or merely setting in motion the 'laws' of mathematics and physics and letting evolution take care of the rest, God infuses the universe and everything in it with God's presence (mind), how might this affect my understanding of the universe and, ultimately, my understanding of human beings?

It seems to me that God has two options from which to choose if God is to be intrinsically involved in the universe. Firstly, God could have created the universe as a simple extension of God-self. That is to say, the universe might be an instrument through which God directly expresses God-self in every detail. From sub-atomic particles all the way through to the most sophisticated life-forms, God could direct the operations of all things rather as a game-master might control the actions of avatars in a virtual reality game. In this scenario, the universe really is a simple extension of God's mind; if we could speak of God having an 'imagination', then we are the products of whatever God chooses to 'imagine'; controlled in our thoughts and actions, down to the finest detail.

If such were the case, then it is true that God would have acted in a manner that might be seen as being infinitely creative. As God chooses to act in and through every part of the universe, God is free to expand infinitely the out-workings of whatever mathematical and physical laws God has chosen to create and this process may continue forever; perhaps forever creating more complex universes, populated with an infinite array of creatures.

While this may be seen as being infinitely creative, it is not, however, *supremely* creative. If God has acted in this way, then God has not created any creatures that are able to act of their own volition, even in a limited way. Any characters or personalities that they might seem to have are, in fact, illusory; they would have no more substance than the characters in a novel or in a film. Such characters would certainly be the products of a creative mind, but it is doubtful that they could be described as being real 'persons'. This would mean, in effect, that 'I' do not really exist in any sense as a thinking person with my own volition. In this scenario, I am as much a slave of determinism as I would be if classical materialism were true and, as with classical materialism, there is no way in which I could know that such is the case. This book, for example, would not be a product of my mind at all, since 'my' mind does not really exist. It would be entirely a product of God's mind even though 'I', mistakenly, think that it reflects 'my' thoughts.

There are major problems with such a proposition. Not only does it make 'my' existence illusory, it also begs the question why God would possibly want to act in such a way. Frankly, it all sounds more than a bit pointless; not a characteristic that I would associate with a Supreme Being. If this were to be true, it also requires God to act out a kind of subterfuge against God-self. I have no awareness that 'I' am really God acting through the bit of the universe that I call my body; again, why would God wish to act in such a manner? Since 'I' and every other person that I know are very fallible and, at times, less than moral individuals, this theory would require God to act out millions of lives in which God gratuitously opposes God's will. All in all, such a theory frankly makes God appear to be quite insane; once more an unlikely characteristic to associate with a Supreme Being.

God *could*, however, act in a way that is *both* infinitely and supremely creative. Since I have suggested that, if God exists, God is a Supreme Being, I expect that this is, in fact, how God has acted. It is possible for God to create and to infuse the universe and everything in it with God's presence, without choosing to direct its development and progress in every respect. There is no need to make God a prisoner of God's own omnipotence.

In other words, God could be 'in' everything, *experiencing* everything that everything experiences, without *directly* causing these experiences to happen. I say, 'directly' because God would still be responsible for the 'laws' of mathematics and physics by which the universe develops and so, would always be 'indirectly' responsible for everything (an important moral point that I shall return to later). God could *also* act within the universe according to other 'laws' governing the nature of the relationship between mind and matter/energy; 'laws' that may be, at least in part, forever beyond our complete comprehension. It is reasonable to suppose that in keeping with what might be expected of a Supreme Being, God would act in a manner that is coherent and consistent, regardless of which 'laws' God has formulated for the existence and development of the universe. From the sub-atomic level, all the way up to the level of sentient creatures, I do not think that this raises any insurmountable philosophical issues, although with the emergence of creatures that might be capable of exercising 'free-will', new questions arise.

At this level, things definitely become more interesting and much more 'creative'; the whole purpose of God creating the universe has now to be considered. If God merely wanted to conduct a massive thought-experiment, without any purpose other than the desire to so act, then the universe would in many ways be meaningless. If, however, God as a Supreme Being, chooses to act with purpose in God's creative actions, then it seems to me to be entirely feasible that one such purpose, *indeed an over-riding moral purpose*, would be to create other beings with minds that would be able to relate to one another and with God at a genuinely personal level. These creatures would emerge from within the universe because God has made the universe in a particular way, but as long as God chooses not to *determine* their thoughts, experiences and choices, then they would be genuinely personal beings in a way similar to the way in which God is a personal being. This would be a *supremely* creative thing to do; indeed, just the sort of thing that I might expect of a Supreme Being. In this way, the universe is not only an 'extension' of God, it is also something that has, within limitations, *its own dynamic* that God undergirds and experiences, but does not direct in every detail. Human beings may then be seen as being strangely God-like; one might even go so far as to say that we are made 'in the image of God'. This does not mean that other creatures, or humans that fail to reach this stage of development, are morally insignificant, but it does indicate that the creation of free, if limited, minds is one essential reason why the universe exists.

Such a view of the nature of the relationship between God and the universe does mean that a degree of indeterminacy has been woven into the universe by God. Indeterminacy is often seen as being a bad thing by some theologians as it implies that God is not 'in control' of everything and hence would not be a Supreme Being. This objection is, however, invalid. Being supreme means that God is in control of whatever God chooses to be in control of. While it is correct to argue that a Supreme Being ought to have complete knowledge of everything that exists, it is not necessary for a Supreme Being directly to *control* everything that exists.

Indeterminacy means that God has chosen an 'open' future for the universe in the sense that human beings and perhaps other similar beings in other parts of the universe write their own stories within the limitations set by their finite natures. For God to allow me to choose which career to pursue, for example, is to allow me to open up a vast array of personal interactions with people that will differ greatly depending on which career I actually pursue. When I think of the myriad of decisions that I make each week and the effects, large and small that those decisions have on other people and when I multiple this by the seven billion or so other people similarly making decisions, I can begin to understand just how supremely creative it is of God to fashion such a universe. If, as might be the case, there are other universes in existence, God's creativity just seems to get bigger and bigger.

What does this type of indeterminacy mean, however, for God's infinite knowledge of everything? Is it possible to say, as I suggested earlier, that God experiences all of time, all of the time, as well as experiencing time through our eyes without this compromising genuine indeterminacy? In other words, if God knows what my entire life consists of because God is experiencing the totality of my life as well as all the parts of it, does this not really mean that my decisions and actions tomorrow are already determined since God knows precisely and totally what they are going to be?

I think that this is a problem only if I were to think that *knowing* the outcome of an event with absolute certainty is the same as *determining* that outcome. I do not believe that such is the case. I have an innate sense that I shall write my own future within the limitations set by my interactions with others, including God. I cannot see that, because God 'already knows' what I am going to decide, my freedom of choice, *when I make it*, is determined in any way. If I make choice 'A', then, of course, when viewing the totality of my life, God will know from God's perspective that choice 'A' was always the only choice that I was going to make. If I were to make choice 'B', then choice 'B' would occupy that position. This does not mean either that God determines which choices I make or that, because God knows which choices I will make, those choices are not freely made by me when I make them.

I have said already, however, that not only does God experience 'all of the balloon' of space and time, but that God also experiences 'every point on the surface of the balloon' and that God does so not merely as an external observer, but rather 'in' the universe. This means that God experiences my decision-making through my eyes, as it were. It also means, I suggest, that when viewing the universe 'from within', God experiences the indeterminacy of decision-making. From '*within*' space/time God does not know my decisions before I make them since God experiences my thoughts alongside me, even though 'apart from' the universe God *does* know what the outcome will be. As I shall explore later, it is important to think of God relating to human beings from both perspectives: 'within' and 'apart from' space/time.

I acknowledge that this is not a thought likely to spring readily to most people's minds. The nature of God's relationship with us does, therefore, some require further exploration.

Chapter Eight

It's Life, but Not As We Know It –
Who or What is God?

(Defining 'Good'… The Necessity of Relationship…
The Place of Humans in the Universe)

In order better to understand the nature of the relationship between God and human beings I think that it is first of all necessary to explore at greater length what sort of being God is. In other words, if I am to think of myself as having a 'relationship' with, or to, God, then I need to be clear what the basis of that relationship is. In particular, I want to explore whether, in some sense, God 'needs' human beings to complete or to fulfil God's existence. Only a deeper understanding of God's nature will, I think, point to the answer to this fundamentally important question.

What Do You Get the Person Who Has Everything?

At some time or other most of us have probably been left scratching our heads, trying desperately to work out what to buy as a birthday present for a relative or friend who seems to have just about everything. It is never an easy task, but if we do manage to emerge from a store clasping the elusive gift to our bosoms we feel a certain sense of triumph. We have managed (we hope) to penetrate the mind of such a self-reliant individual and we have come up with the goods! If God, however, is not simply a magnified version of this, but really is a being who is 'missing' nothing and who is totally, completely and absolutely self-possessed, self-reliant and self-everything-else, how might this inform my understanding of what God is like?

I have already argued that while viewing God as a Supreme Being indicates that God is 'complete', this does not mean that God must be, or have to do, everything imaginable. To be supreme, God does not have to be evil or to engage in torture. God is complete in that God has everything that God chooses to have and God has nothing that God chooses not to have. Anything that may reasonably be seen as being 'good' or 'worth having' or 'giving meaning, value, purpose or dignity', God will possess in and of God-self. While acknowledging that I am working within the limits of language and the limits of human concepts, nonetheless, I think that it is reasonable to say that if God is a Supreme Being, God ought to possess the type of qualities, characteristics and attributes that are signified in the above list. If God were to be 'missing' any of these, or similar things, then God would not be a Supreme Being.

A question immediately pops into my mind, however: who decides what is 'good' or 'positive'? The answer, of course, has to be 'God'. If this were not so, then someone or something other than God would be in control of deciding what is, or is not, good or positive and if someone or something other than God is in control of this, then God cannot be a Supreme Being. Is this not, however, simply sending me round in circles? If God decides what is good or positive and, furthermore, if God cannot be lacking anything good or positive, is this just not another way of saying that God chooses whatever God chooses to choose and that, by definition, becomes 'good'? If it were to be claimed that God could have chosen chaos to be 'positive' or the murder of innocents 'good', then I have to admit that, in principle, such could have been the case.

In purely abstract terms, God could be quite the opposite from the way God is. In theological terms, however, this is not the case. I have already argued that one reason I am able to speak meaningfully about God is that God chooses to reveal God-self to humans. While, *theoretically*, God might have revealed God-self to be nasty, brutish and vindictive, theology suggests that God has revealed God-self as being good, loving and compassionate and that these concepts are both meaningful and important to us. They form part of what I consider a Supreme Being to manifest; if anyone wishes to assert that evil or gratuitous unpredictability ought to be part of a Supreme Being's character and nature, he or she is free to make that case. It is not one, however, that commends itself to me, regardless of the theoretical possibility that it might be true.

Similarly, if it is suggested that good things only appear to be 'good' to us because that is the way God has made us to interpret life, then it must be accepted that such is indeed the case, but that this perception of life is one that makes sense. It is difficult, if not impossible, to see how a universe in which gratuitous suffering, inflicted on the weak by the powerful, could be seen as a 'good thing'. At some point I have to accept that my perception and understanding of reality is what it is and those things that I consider to be 'good' such as love, and integrity, are, indeed, good. Again, the floor is open to anyone who wishes to argue a contrary case. What this all means is that God, as a Supreme Being will not be 'missing' anything that is good or positive and God as a Supreme Being will not 'have' anything bad or negative.

Relationship

One of the things that I consider to be 'good' is relationship. Of course, not all relationships are good and few, if any, relationships are good all the time. Nonetheless, the experience of relationship: the ability to give and to receive, to communicate, to love and to enjoy companionship, I view as being a positive thing. While some people may prefer solitude to socializing, it is doubtful that even these people believe that the best possible option for them is to be absolutely alone in the universe. With regard to God, however, is relationship also an essential 'good'? If it is, then it is something that God must not be 'missing' in and of God-self. If this is the case, then it has profound implications for my understanding of God.

Could absolute solitude be possible for a Supreme Being? On the one hand a Supreme Being does not need any other being or thing for anything. If another being or thing is *necessary* in any sense, then God is no longer a Supreme Being. On the other hand, however, it is clear that in creating the universe, God has also created a nexus of relationships, not only including inter-personal relationships within the universe, but also, relationship between God-self and God's creation. Furthermore, *relationship*, if not necessarily all relationships, is correctly deemed by most people to be a good thing in itself, and hence something that God must 'have'.

So, it appears that there is something of a conundrum to untangle. God must be self-sufficient and not in need of relationship with anyone or anything else and yet in creating the universe, God has initiated relationship both within the universe and between God-self and persons within the universe. As relationship is a good and positive thing, has God created something that God was otherwise missing? If God has, then God is no longer a Supreme Being, though God would still be a very powerful being.

There are, I think, five main ways of trying to resolve this problem. The first is to say that relationship is *not* a good or positive thing and so God need not experience relationship 'apart from' the universe. This, surely, is highly problematic. If I substitute the word 'relationship' with the term 'love', it becomes even more of a problem. Can love (which, of course can only be experienced and expressed in relationship) really not be a good thing? I might argue, in theory, that such may be the case but such an argument is, frankly, unconvincing. I cannot *prove* that love is a 'good' thing but, on balance, it is much more reasonable to believe that it is than that it is not. Of course, relationships may also give rise to hurt and pain, but this does not mean that relationship itself is either a bad or even a neutral thing. The things that give rise to hurt and pain are, in fact, negations of relationship. It is refusal to relate or refusal to relate in a positive way that causes suffering in relationships, not the existence of relationship itself. Claiming that relationship (or love) is not an intrinsically good thing and hence not something that God must be able to experience 'apart from' the universe might be theoretically possible but, in reality, it is an unsatisfactory solution to the problem.

A second approach is to argue that God is absolutely solitary 'apart from' the universe and that God remains solitary even with the universe in existence. In other words, God does not relate to the universe or to any persons within it. God simply created the universe and has left it to its own devices. This theory, often termed, 'deism', has always held an appeal for some philosophers and scientists, but a little thought exposes its weaknesses. It requires me to accept that relationship (love) is either not a 'good' thing or, if it is a good thing, that God has chosen to withhold something good from creation (God's love), since God has chosen not to relate with creation, thereby denying it an ultimate value that it could otherwise have had. It also begs the question: what is the point of the universe? If it is nothing more than the disinterested creation of a non-relating God, then it really is of very little significance. Is it reasonable to suppose that God chose to engage in a pointless exercise of creation? Again, this could all be true, but if it is, it leaves me with a Supreme Being that looks suspiciously low on moral responsibility and high on pointlessness; hardly attributes to be expected of a Supreme Being.

A third option is to argue that God might, indeed, be conceived of as a solitary Supreme Being, but that creativity is such an *intrinsic* part of God's nature that creation, in some form, exists alongside God as an *eternal* reality. This is not the same thing as saying that God chose a very long time ago, to create something extrinsic to God-self. Rather, it is to say that God, by virtue of God's very nature, does not exist apart from God's own creativity. In so far as I can talk in terms of 'time' when speaking of eternity, I might then say that just as God is eternal, so too is God's creativity and so too is some form of 'creation'. While that creation is not likely to be our universe, which appears to have had a beginning, it would be something or someone that I might think of as '*always existing*' just as God has always existed *and because* God has always existed. In this sense, relationship might *theoretically* be seen as being something 'external' to God, but, *in effect*, it is something that *inevitably and eternally* exists as part of God's self-expression. 'Creation' and God at the most fundamental level possible are inseparable.

To pursue this thought further, I might say that God's creative nature is such that God's creative self-expression has taken two essential forms. The first is an eternal form and the second is a temporal form. The first might mirror God's *essential* nature perfectly and, in crude terms, could be thought of almost as self-replication (I am *painfully* aware of the inadequacies of language at this point and the need to remember that all language is analogous). Out of and from this 'essential' creativity could flow 'temporal creation'; perhaps a never-ending sequence and variety of universes stretching into eternity. The difference between 'essential creation' and 'temporal creation' are such, that it might be better to employ two totally different terms to describe them. As I write, I cannot but think of the biblical terminology of 'the Logos' being 'begotten' of God and as Christ being 'the first-born of Creation', but I am aware that I am running ahead of my own enquiry.

A fourth approach, which could be viewed as a refinement of that above, leads me into relatively unchartered waters and introduces a distinctive way of viewing God. Just as I have already spoken of classical and dynamic theism, this approach might be described as *mystical theism* (in effect, a particular way of viewing dynamic theism). The essential concept is that while God might be conceived of as a single unitary Supreme Being, God's inherent creativity *and love* are such that God's 'end-purpose' is to unite with God's creation, or at least with those parts of creation that wish to be united with God. While any such unity will take place *within* time, God's *experience* of this unity will be eternal. Because this is so, those beings that are united with God will, in some sense, have been 'with' God eternally; their actions in time will have 'retro-active' effect because of *God's* eternal nature. In this way, because of God's *essential* creativity and love, God will 'always' have experienced relationship. I accept that this strains both language and imagination to the limit, although no more so than philosophical reflections fuelled by modern theories in physics and cosmology. This approach to addressing the nature of the relationship between God and creation suggests that God has eternally enjoyed relationship because of God's *inherent* creativity and because of God's *intrinsic* love for creation. The 'supreme' nature of God's existence is not put at risk, because creation is inherently an outworking of one aspect of *God's* character and is intrinsically bound to God in the deepest possible way. In *mystical theism*, it is not possible to view those parts of creation that are 'bound' to God as being *existentially* extrinsic to God because God has *eternally* bound them to God-self. While I accept that this concept might not be easy to 'follow through' on the basis of reason alone, I find that intuitively it resonates within me. Consequently, I am prepared to view it as *one* viable and defensible way of understanding the nature of God, albeit one that I suspect I shall never come close to fathoming rationally; hence the term, *mystical theism*.

A fifth way of approaching this problem (which may be seen as a refinement of one or more of the previous approaches or which may be seen as standing alone) is to say that God, *without reference to anyone or to anything else*, eternally and essentially, enjoys relationship *in God-self*. This is different from postulating a number of divine beings relating to one another (polytheism) since this would negate the concept of a Supreme Being. It is also different from postulating a being with a single, undifferentiated 'consciousness', quite alone 'apart from' creation. What I am referring to is a single, truly Supreme Being, with a 'communal' or 'multi-centred' consciousness enjoying relationship essentially and intrinsically within God-self, 'apart from' the universe, while also relating to persons within the universe. That 'multi-centred consciousness' could be simply the way God is, or it could be a result of God's 'essential creation' as outlined above.

Either way, I might think that this does not sound like any person that I know and I would be right; God, after all, really is in a category of one. It is for this reason that I have said that, in theology, the concept of what a 'person' is ought to come from a concept of God, not from a concept of human persons. It is clear that I cannot hope to come close to appreciating the person that God is if I continue to think of God as a bigger version of me. I can, however, understand myself and others as 'reflections' of what God is. God experiences communal personality; I experience simple personality. God experiences 'internal' relationship; I experience external relationship. God experiences total self-sufficient love; I experience dependent and partial love. The 'real' person is God but it has to be said that I and others do not fare so badly as God's somewhat pale reflections.

Does such a 'communal' or 'multi-centred' person make sense? I think that, not only does it make sense; it has the potential to form an essential part of how I might view God if God is indeed, a Supreme Being. While it is quite impossible for me to understand fully what God is like 'apart from' the universe, I can see no difficulty in God being a 'community' of personal interaction, with distinct, but *entirely overlapping* centres of thought, will and expression existing in perfect, mutual knowledge, communication and love. Without perfect, mutual knowledge, communication and love I should be talking of 'gods' rather than God, but a communal being within which there is total and absolutely perfect, mutual knowledge, communication and love is, in fact, a single being, not a plurality of beings. This is, I acknowledge, an initially strange concept, but if I think of the various 'personal centres' within God as being infinite and also as being in absolute and perfect 'overlap' with one another, what I should see is perfect unity, perfect 'oneness'. A being that is 'multi-centred', with each personal 'focus' in full and absolute relationship with each other 'focus', sharing total knowledge and love, cannot be anything other than a single 'communal' being. If there was only partial sharing in relationship or if there was any withholding of knowledge or love, then I might speak of inter-related beings, but in the context of absolute and total relationship, 'communal personality' in a single being is the appropriate way to begin to 'describe' God.

If as I have suggested, relationship is 'good', then if God is a Supreme Being, God must either be such a 'communal being' or a being akin to that outlined in the previous two concepts, or a combination of two or more of them. A 'communal' understanding of God certainly addresses the need for God, intrinsically to have the 'good' of relationship within God-self. It also helps me to understand how 'goodness' is an intrinsic aspect of God's character; I find it easier to appreciate 'goodness' or 'morality' as being a necessary characteristic of a communal being than of a 'simple' unitary being.

What About Us?

All of this sets the relationship between God and creation in a distinctive light. God has not created the universe as an extrinsic 'thing', to fill some sort of personal void, as if God got lonely after spending a few aeons on God's own. Why then, did God create the universe at all?

While God could not be a Supreme Being if God had to create the universe in order to satisfy a need that could only be met extrinsically by someone or something 'outside' of God, God could still be a Supreme Being if God created the universe as an expression of God's innate character and nature. In other words, *if creativity lies at the very heart of God's nature*, then as an inevitable consequence of God's own nature, the universe (or universes, or multi-verse) *had* to come into existence. This is not to say that God had to act creatively because of some externally imposed imperative, rather it acknowledges that certain inevitable consequences follow from God's *intrinsic* nature, a nature that is determined by God and no-one else. If, as I think it is reasonable to propose, creativity is 'good', then, as I have already stated, God will be infinitely and supremely creative since God is infinitely and supremely good. Neither God's goodness nor creativity can be limited if God is supreme. The universe, a good and creative expression of God, could no more *not exist* than God could not be creative. While the universe is entirely contingent upon God, given God's nature, *its existence is entirely assured*.

Some physicists and cosmologists have suggested that either multiple universes or a 'multi-verse' containing all possible universes, exist. This is sometimes viewed as being contrary to theism, but such is not necessarily the case. A 'multi-verse', understood as containing *all possible* universes would, indeed, be problematic since 'all possible universes' would include universes that are utterly chaotic and 'lawless', set alongside universes that are eternal and without a creator, as well as universes in which such things as torture and murder are viewed by sentient beings as being 'good'. It would, indeed, be difficult, if not impossible, to reconcile this understanding of a 'multi-verse' with the existence of a Supreme Being. Multiple universes, either existing alongside one another or existing sequentially, is, however, a different proposition. I can see no reason why such multiple universes ought not to exist in parallel with one another, unless it could be demonstrated that 'our' universe is the only possible 'good' universe that could be created. Even if such were the case, it is entirely possible (given an expanded understanding of time and space) that our universe has been 'preceded' by earlier universes and will be 'succeeded' by later ones. I am not arguing that multiple universes are *necessary* in order for God to be supremely creative, but that they pose no threat to theism and may, in fact, enhance whatever *theodigm* might emerge from my enquiry.

Since God is 'mind', all that has been created is an expression of mind. Quite literally, *if God exists*, it is correct to say that everything that exists, exists entirely and purely in the mind of God. This expression may appear to suggest that the universe is, therefore, in some sense not real; it exists 'only in the mind'. To think along these lines, however, would be to fall into the perennial trap of thinking of God as being just a bigger version of human beings. As a Supreme Being, the 'mind of God' is ultimate and complete reality; there is no existence apart from the mind of God and the mind of God encompasses all that exists. It is the mind of God that has not only created the universe and sustains its continued existence, it is also the mind of God that sustains my continued existence as a personal being. It is also the mind of God that could make possible, though not inevitable, my continued existence after my physical death. Clearly, there is much here to explore and I wish to begin by trying to understand better the nature of God's relationship to me.

If, as I have suggested, God did not simply light the fuse that started the Big Bang, but continues to infuse the universe and everything in it, then what implications does this have for me? In the first instance, I can understand my existence as a thinking, feeling, perceiving person as being the result of my biological development which, in turn, is the result of processes of 'theistic' evolution which owe their efficacy, not simply to a mixture of time and chance, but to the very precise 'laws' and interactions that God has established that make the universe's existence and evident order possible. *If God exists*, I do not believe that I exist as a 'soul' that has been fused with a body, nor do I believe that I am a purely material entity that operates according to fixed and determined processes. The fact that my mind has emerged because my brain is sufficiently complex to allow this to happen and that this is possible because the matter/energy of my brain is a manifestation of a Fundamental Mind (God), makes it possible to say that something new has emerged that goes beyond what I or others may term the 'physical'.

Once matter/energy has become so ordered that it can make the existence of individual minds possible, there are, as I outlined earlier, two possibilities for God to pursue. God could act directly in and through human brains and minds in a manner that enables God to express God-self directly in the various circumstances and events of human lives. In this scenario, I would be a direct extension of God with every thought, action and perception being God's thought, action and perception in the context of my particular human life. Although this may be seen as corresponding well with what I earlier termed 'idealist emergence', I have already stated why I believe that God is unlikely to have acted in this way. If, however, there was sufficient reason, God could choose to act in this manner in a more limited fashion. It is entirely possible that God could act directly in and as a human mind, *in a given individual* as long as this was not a charade and that individual, within the limitations of human experience, had a sense of 'identity' with God. To do so with *every* human being, however, would be to suggest that God has failed to act in a supremely creative manner by failing to bring into existence other minds that enjoy sufficient freedom and limited autonomy, able to have genuinely free relationships with other minds and with God.

By combining emergence theory with dynamic theism, it is, however, possible to see how God could be 'in' every human life without directly controlling it. If *dynamic emergence* were true, then the mind that emerges from a human brain would be wholly accessible to God since everything that exists is an 'emanation' from God, made from 'God-stuff' rather than being made from a different substance called 'matter'. It is not difficult to see how such minds could have sufficient moral independence from God to allow them to make independent decisions, in particular to be able to make morally significant decisions including whether or not to relate positively to God; a pre-requisite in a genuinely 'good' relationship. If *idealist emergence* were true, then the mental or mind-field that permeates the universe is also an emanation from God and, as such, provides a ready means of God being 'in' every human being without thereby exercising direct control. In either case, God could have full and complete knowledge of all other minds, understanding their every thought, decision and perception as well as the various influences on them. God would still be present, with and in every human being, but not present as a determining factor in their decision making.

Clearly, if any of the above approximates to reality, I must be aware that when I speak of 'God's mind' I am not simply speaking of a bigger version of a human mind. I must be careful not to fall into the trap of thinking that God thinks as I do, only in a deeper and faster way. The mind of God is *pure mind* and all other minds exist within it; the distinction between my mind and God's mind being infinitely greater than that between an abacus and the world's most advanced computer.

I have made much of the desirability of God (if God exists) creating individual personal beings within the universe that are free to make moral and relational choices, particularly the choice whether or not to relate positively to God. Why this is so important, what its implications are for the sort of universe that God is thereby 'free' to create and how this places limits on the ways in which God may relate to humans is the topic of the next chapter.

Chapter Nine

The Price of Freedom – Human Morality
(Non-coercion in Belief... Revelation... Human Freedom)

I have already suggested that *if God exists*, it is reasonable to believe that, as a Supreme Being, God is both supremely good and supremely creative. It is also reasonable to believe that God would demonstrate these qualities by creating minds that are themselves, capable of being creative and that have sufficient autonomy to make moral decisions, including decisions about whether or not they want to relate positively to God and to one another. I now want to add the thought that bringing such creatures into existence is the *essential* reason why the universe exists and why it exists in the form in which it does. I cannot think of anything more supremely good or creative than for God to express God-self in such a way that semi-autonomous, genuinely moral, creative beings come into existence. While absolute autonomy is not possible as all things must remain dependent upon God for their existence, being 'semi-autonomous' does not impinge negatively upon human beings' *moral* autonomy.

Bringing human beings into existence is supremely creative as it creates infinite opportunities for us to exercise our own creativity, particularly if, as may be the case, our minds might be enabled to survive the dissolution of our bodies. If other minds exist in other solar systems, galaxies or universes, this simply adds to God's creativity. Creating human minds is supremely good in that bringing into existence minds that are able to make moral and relational decisions is supremely altruistic. For God to create minds that are free to decide how to relate to God is, in my view, both breathtakingly daring and lavishly magnanimous. It also carries with it self-imposed limitations on what sort of universe or universes God could create as well as limitations on how God may relate to moral creatures once they have emerged.

At the heart of morality lies freedom to make autonomous decisions, regardless of external influences or internal limitations. For example, I can clearly recall one of the earliest moral dilemmas that I faced as a child. I was around seven or eight years old and was taking part in a PE class at school. The teacher was known to have a sharp and somewhat unpredictable temper; he was also less than innovative in his approach to physical education. On one particular occasion, he formed all the members of the class into two lines about ten metres apart and partnered us off. He then handed a tennis ball to each pair and instructed us to throw and catch. At that age, I was not particularly well-coordinated and was likely to drop or to miss as many throws as I would catch. My problem, on this occasion was that I was standing with my back to an area of long, uncut grass and wild shrubs. There was a distinct possibility that a ball that eluded my grasp would disappear into the tangled mass, never to be found, bringing the teacher's wrath upon my head. This thought did nothing to assist my coordination and, inevitably, after a short while the ball whizzed past my left ear. As I turned to see if I could find where it had landed, my worst fears were realised; the ball was nowhere to be seen. I knew that this would result in the teacher 'bawling me out' in a manner akin to a drill-sergeant addressing a recruit who had failed to secure the safety catch on his rifle (happily, schools are different today). As I searched through the grass with mounting feelings of desperation another hapless child missed his ball and it landed close to me. To my shame, I snatched it up and, pretending that it was my own, I returned to the 'game'. The other child, of course, could not find his ball and was subsequently shouted at by the teacher, leaving him humiliated and close to tears. The genuine remorse that I felt did not, however, cause me to own up to my misdemeanour and my discomfort was heightened by the fact that I subsequently found my ball, rendering the whole incident unnecessary.

I felt genuinely miserable for the rest of the day and later, at home, that evening I confessed the whole sorry business to my parents. They were sympathetic, in fact they were too sympathetic, pointing out that it was not my fault that the teacher had intimidated me and that, in any case, no harm was done since the ball was found. I appreciated their solidarity, but I knew that they were wrong. I had made a moral choice, albeit under pressure and within my limited abilities as an eight year old, but a moral choice nonetheless. What is more, I had made the wrong choice. The event, and the lessons I learned from it, have stayed with me ever since; I still wince at my actions, even now. Sadly, I cannot remember the other child's name, but if by some bizarre chance he ever reads this book, I wish to offer my sincere apologies.

The point of this story is to illustrate that even though we may have limited abilities to analyse our actions and even though we may be pressured by others to act in certain ways, in the end there is almost always a genuine decision to be made and it is this ability to make decisions that makes us moral beings. If, however, my abilities were so limited that I was unable to make a decision or if I were so pressured that I had no real freedom to choose, then my actions would be amoral. For this reason, very small children are not held responsible for their actions and people who act under duress are usually treated leniently by the law.

If God is to act in a manner that is both supremely creative and supremely good, then God must act in such a way that humans have sufficient ability to make moral decisions while not being placed under influences that would invalidate any decisions that are made. This, I believe, is quite a tall order; so tall, that it may be the case that it requires not only a whole universe to accomplish it, but that it might even require our particular universe to accomplish it.

The nub of the problem is this: God is unique and God's nature is such that once God's existence is acknowledged by other minds it carries implications that are unique. Among these implications is the crucial issue of how to relate to a Supreme Being. Frankly, I cannot believe that if I were to come to the conclusion that a Supreme Being exists, I really have any genuine choice in the matter. I have indicated that a Supreme Being is, among other things, supremely creative and supremely good. Such a being is also supremely powerful and supremely knowledgeable. It is one thing to believe that such a being does not exist or to be uncertain about the issue; it is quite another to be *convinced* that such a being does exist and then to decide to carry on with one's life regardless. In essence, I wish to propose that to act in this way would be quite impossible for most human beings. If God exists, God must allow belief to be a genuine human choice; otherwise God will have failed to create truly moral beings.

I am not suggesting that it is impossible to believe in the existence of some superhuman power or being and then choose either to ignore or even to oppose it. People do this all the time. I have lost count of the times that I have said to atheists that I don't believe in the god they don't believe in or to theists that I don't believe in the god that they do believe in. Such a god, whether 'promoted' by atheists or theists is almost invariably something that falls well short of being a Supreme Being. If I did believe in the existence of a limited superhuman power or being it would be a relatively simple matter for me to believe that this entity might not require much from me or it might even be open to negotiation with regard to my behaviour. My earlier comments about individuals accepting or rejecting *theodigms*, rather than accepting or rejecting God, still stand.

Belief in a Supreme Being, however, requires much more from me, even though I may never fully understand or properly appreciate such a being. If I seriously believe that a supremely good, creative, powerful and knowledgeable being exists I cannot see how I can do other than elect to relate to such a being in whatever manner that being might choose. I would do so, on the understanding, of course, that a Supreme Being would only choose what is best for me, in the context of what is best for my fellow human beings and the rest of the universe. In other words, once I *truly* believe that God exists, I am no longer free to reject God's existence or its significance for me. After all, if God exists and I exist 'in God', and if I believe such to be the case, how could I possibly try to live apart from God? Since, as a Supreme Being, God is supremely good, supremely creative and supremely powerful, how could I choose to ignore or to oppose God?

Believing in God as a Supreme Being is akin to believing that the Earth is round. Once I believe that such is the case, I can no longer act as if it were really flat. I might not always be consciously aware of the effects of the Earth's shape on me, but I would know that my existence and my experience of life depend on the Earth being round. To use another analogy, believing that God exists is like believing that one plus one equals two in decimal arithmetic. Once I accept this, other mathematical truths follow inevitably. I cannot argue that one plus one equals two and that two plus two equals five.

The important point of all of this is that, if God is going to create semi-autonomous moral persons then God must make belief in God's existence as a Supreme Being *neither* inevitable nor impossible. If either were the case, I should be unable to make a genuinely free decision whether or not to relate positively to God. This, I suggest, is the most fundamental decision that I can make since everything else in my life is bound to follow from it. In particular, if God's existence was self-evident to all humans, I should have no freedom to choose good over against evil, and without such a choice, I cannot see how I could be, in any sense, a moral being. If God exists, there must, therefore, be *sufficient but not compelling* grounds for belief. Of course, in coming to a decision with regard to belief in God, I will do so, on the basis of my appreciation of various *theodigms*, rather than on direct knowledge of God as God is in God-self. This is precisely why such a decision ought to be subject to continual investigation and re-assessment.

I think that this gives God very little 'wriggle room' indeed. In the first instance it means that there can never be formal logical or scientific proof of God's existence or of God's non-existence. If such were the case, then genuine moral choice has been removed. Since people have always debated whether or not God exists and have further disagreed with regard to what God might be like if God were to exist, it looks as if these fundamental criteria for God creating semi-autonomous moral persons have been met. Allowing genuine choice in belief necessitates God creating an incredibly finely balanced universe in which God's existence may be inferred, but in which it is not self-evident, at least in formal logical or scientific terms. As I shall explore later, certainty of belief for some individuals may be possible because of their experiences or because of the role intuition plays in their personalities. Such certainty, perhaps more properly described as *confidence*, is not proof and never can be seen as such, as any self-respecting sceptic will be quick to point out.

Revelation

What I have been discussing so far in this chapter, theologians often term 'revelation', the question of God's self-disclosure to the human race. If I am correct in arguing that God, as a supremely good and creative being, creates semi-autonomous moral beings and that this defines the sort of universe that God may create, then it also defines God's self-disclosure at every level. In other words, by God's own choice, God is not free to reveal God's existence to human beings in such a way as to deny moral choice to us. This means that God will not act in such a way as to coerce belief or in such a way as to make belief unreasonable; again, a tall order to meet.

If God exists, and if God is 'in' all parts of the universe, God is also 'in' every human being. As I have already outlined, this does not mean that God controls me, but that God has absolute and total 'access' to me, understanding my every thought, feeling and action. Among other things, God has absolute access to my mind and, if God is understood as a Fundamental Mind, my mind may be seen as existing 'in' God and hence, able to have limited access to God's mind. In order for me to act as a truly moral being, God must be present with me in such a way that I am not forced to believe in God's existence, but also in such a way that belief is reasonable. Ways in which God might achieve this, are for me to have some innate moral sense, some innate sense of 'the spiritual' and some innate interest in exploring, intellectually or emotionally, significant questions of life. If God exists, and I am part of a universe that is an expression of God, then it seems reasonable to me that these 'reflections' of God would be present in me. Their presence would not make belief in God inevitable, but they would make it possible. It is also reasonable to believe that I am not the only person on the planet with these aptitudes, but that these are things common to the human race and thereby shared by all human beings to some extent.

Recent theories in brain lateralization suggest that while our whole brains are involved in almost everything that we do, the left and right hemispheres play distinctive roles in enabling us to experience and to understand reality. The left hemisphere of my brain is associated with such things as logic and language; the right with such things as intuition and creativity. If I were to ponder (as I often do) on the conundrum of where my thoughts come from, I should have to admit that I really do not know. I am aware of some of the processes that I employ in thinking, but why certain thoughts occur to me or why answers to certain questions seem to pop into my mind, I cannot always say. What I can say, with some degree of confidence, is that my thoughts emerge from within the whole mental experience *facilitated* by my brain and, in turn, they influence the ways in which my brain enables me to continue to engage in further reflection. The process is ongoing, forming a kind of mental spiral in which my mind and my brain interact with one another, building complex 'strings' of thought and reflection. The end-point of a particular thought might be an 'articulation' utilising language, but there is more to a thought than this end product.

For example, when I am in conversation I might choose to respond to a statement made by another person with humour, with empathy or with an intellectual challenge. The context of the conversation and the nature of my relationship with the other person will help to indicate which approach I am likely to take. The actual words that come out of my mouth, however, are likely to follow almost immediately upon a thought, which I rapidly filter before articulating. The thought itself, however, most often simply 'appears' in my mind; I am seldom consciously aware of piecing it together or of constructing it from a series of earlier thoughts. Nonetheless, something like this must happen at a sub-conscious level, otherwise the thought could never get to the stage at which I can 'filter' and then choose to articulate it. In this process, there is interplay between the right, 'affective' part of my brain and the left 'logical' part of my brain.

I suggest that there is ample opportunity for God's mind to be one, non-determining factor in this process. I am *not* suggesting that God pops thoughts into my head, but rather, since my mind exists in the mind of God and since my mind is fully accessible to God, that the right hemisphere of my brain has developed in such a way that it may be attuned to subtle influences in *my* mind that contribute to the creation of an innate moral sense, an innate spiritual sense and an innate desire to explore the significance of my and other lives. The left side of my brain will try to 'make sense' of this and enable me to produce reasoned arguments which will (I hope) contain inherent logic, but which are influenced by the innate 'aptitudes' that I have outlined above. Just as my mind is able to respond to the physical environment around me because my brain is able to interpret a multitude of sensory data with which it is bombarded, so too, my mind is able to respond to, to interpret and to engage with the mental or spiritual environment in which it exists because my brain is equipped to facilitate this process.

I am not suggesting that the presence of these aptitudes is proof of God's existence; there are, undoubtedly, alternative explanations for them. I am proposing, however, that *if God exists*, these may form the basis for my relating to God. They indicate ways in which God may reveal God-self to me and ways in which I may respond to that revelation. By their very nature, they are personal to each individual and so, no matter how confident one individual may be with regard to the question of God's existence, that confidence will never be able to have much more than a peripheral influence on another person. If God exists, this too, is part of the fine-tuning that is required for belief to be a genuinely free choice.

Nonetheless, I should also expect that human beings will talk to one another about their questions and beliefs and that some will even talk of their perceived 'experiences' of God. Because we are, by and large, communal creatures, it is also reasonable to suppose that through a process of discourse, experimentation and enculturation those who come to believe in God's existence will congregate around commonly held beliefs, insights and interpretations. They will write down what they and their communities regard as especially important teachings or texts, they will formalise certain expressions of worship, ethics and conduct and they will, inevitably, have disputes with those who disagree with them. In short, they will develop religions. Those who conclude that God does not exist will, similarly, engage in disputes, proposing various alternatives to religion while often being irritated by the whole notion that others believe in God's existence at all. If God exists, and if God wishes to create truly moral beings, such a plethora of opinion and practice is to be expected.

For us to be truly moral beings, however, more than freedom of belief is necessary; we must also have freedom of practice. If God exists, God will not intervene in human interactions in any way that is coercive, thereby enforcing belief in God's existence. Equally, God will not be so remote from human interactions that belief in God's existence would be unreasonable; for example, our behaviour cannot be a matter of moral indifference to God. This means, I believe, that human beings must be given an almost frightening ability to act for good or for evil in our relationships with one another, without, at the same time, being permitted to descend into absolute moral chaos. Without such freedom to act, I cannot see how we can be moral creatures and yet, if we were to descend into moral oblivion I cannot see how belief in God would be tenable. I must, therefore, have a genuine moral choice to make between good and evil, while at the same time, recognising that good is morally preferable to evil.

What this means, I believe, is that throughout human history as well as in my personal relationships, I expect to see both evil and good being done, but undergirding this moral ebb and flow there ought to be a *widely held* conviction that good is greater than evil and that good will ultimately triumph. This conviction might sound almost impossibly idealistic, but if God exists, I should expect God's influence in human lives to be such that good will keep breaking through human selfishness, nastiness and evil. This will not always be evident in every instance, but I should expect it to be a general and recognisable trend. Such, I suggest, is indeed, the case. We human beings, in spite of multiple reasons to act selfishly are, as a species, strangely oriented towards recognising and pursuing good; something that is borne out, against all odds, in history and in the billions of inter-personal relationships throughout the world. As I have acknowledged, good does not triumph in every case, but the pursuit of good is not to be denied even in the darkest of places and circumstances. Again, this does not prove God's existence; it is, however, *compatible* with such belief.

In this understanding of the way in which God relates to human beings, the whole point of life appears to be that it enables our existence as moral, creative beings. It is not necessary for me to believe in God or in a particular *theodigm* to be able to recognise that good is morally preferable to evil, even if I fail to live up to this insight in my own life. I am, it seems, incapable of pursuing good exclusively and so I all too frequently, think and act in ways that hurt other people. I do feel, though, that I have a genuine freedom to choose my basic moral orientation and that this choice is of significance. What this indicates, I suggest, is that *if God exists*, God's ultimate interest in us is as moral, creative beings that may choose, not so much to *be* good, but to *desire to be good*. In allowing us this freedom, God not only bestows on us a unique moral status, but God also has created beings that have the potential either to be agents of great good or of great evil within the universe. This has, I believe, the most profound implications both for us and for God.

Chapter Ten

Taking Responsibility Seriously –
The Consequences of Creation

(Incarnation… Sinless Living?… The Death of God-Incarnate…
Incarnation and 'Mystical' Theism)

I suggested earlier, that in creating humans as genuinely moral beings, God has acted in a supremely good way. If God is a 'communal personality', God does not need human beings in order to enjoy relationship, but as a supremely creative being God has chosen to exercise creativity in a supremely altruistic way, by giving existence to a multitude of semi-autonomous beings that are also able to be both good and creative, if they so choose. It is difficult to see how God could have acted in a more creative way or in a way that has within it greater capacity for good to emerge.

There is, however, a problem with this; indeed so large a problem that it has caused many people to reject or to abandon belief in God's existence. While creating humans as genuinely moral beings has the capacity for great good to ensue, it has also resulted in great suffering and distress both for humans and for other species. In spite of our innate orientation towards recognising and pursuing good we also have an appalling record of inflicting pain and embracing evil. If God exists and if God is supremely good, this cannot be a matter of indifference to God, nor can it simply be swept under the celestial carpet by claiming that the good in the universe outweighs the evil.

One problem with such a calculation is that it is by no means certain that if it were possible to set, side by side, all the good and all the evil deeds done in human history that good would, in fact, come out on top. The greater problem, however, is that, on principle, such an exercise is entirely impossible. Good and evil are not commodities to be counted like apples or home appliances. They may be the antithesis of one another, but neither I, nor anyone else, is able properly to quantify them or to devise a formula by which they may be weighed against each other. Moral arithmetic does not exist. How much good is needed to outweigh a particular evil deed? How, for example, can I compare the evil of the holocaust with the good of eradicating smallpox? It simply cannot be done.

I think that I am on reasonably firm ground when I assert that if I find such an idea morally bankrupt, God is unlikely to have set God-self a lower standard. If good is going to overcome evil in the universe, then it must do so in such a way that evil is thereby transformed, not, merely 'outweighed'. As God is supremely good and supremely wise, (should God exist) God will both understand and accept all the implications of creating semi-autonomous moral beings. Chief among those implications is the need to address the issue of how evil might be overcome by good so that creating moral beings is, in fact, a morally good thing to do. As evil is an inevitable consequence of God's decision to create morally autonomous beings within the universe, God cannot be thought of as acting morally unless God is also able to ensure that evil is overcome. Of course, if God has not acted morally, God cannot be a Supreme Being.

For this reason, it would be insufficient for God simply to create a universe that neither demanded nor prohibited belief in God in order that we could make a moral choice to pursue good, *and then to leave us to our own devices*. For God to be good and to be seen to be good, greater involvement with the human race is necessary. God, being a Supreme Being, will not only be involved in the human race in such a way that evil is overcome by good, but God will be involved with the human race in a *supremely* good and creative way; a way that is true to God's intrinsic character. This means that, *should God exist*, God must act in such a manner that evil is overcome in an ultimate and final way, while maintaining the fine balance between making belief in God neither inevitable nor unreasonable. Yet again, this is a tall order to meet.

Incarnation

In order to be supremely good, I suggest that it is not *sufficient* for God to understand and to know everything about human suffering and the consequences of human evil. No matter how close God might be to me, living, as it were, my life *alongside* me, this is not the same as God *experiencing* human suffering and the consequences of human evil for God-self. This omission, unless addressed, is critical as it consigns human beings, as moral persons, *to facing the consequences of God's creative actions in a manner that God does not.* This, it seems to me, would be unjust. I would not ask my children to endure something as a consequence of my actions, that, if possible, I would not seek to endure myself; I cannot imagine that my sense of justice is more finely tuned that God's. To be truly supreme, God must not only know about human life, but must surely also have to *experience* human suffering and the consequences of human evil. While it is undoubtedly true that human evil must cause God, the Creator, pain in a unique way, this is still not the same as God *identifying directly* with the suffering of God's own creation. That can only be done *as a human being*. I find it difficult to believe that anything less than this is worthy of a Supreme Being or that anything less than this demonstrates that God is prepared to take absolute responsibility for God's creation of moral beings. 'Where is God?' has been the cry on the lips of countless suffering people; unless God has *experienced* human suffering it is difficult to view any possible answer as providing more than a platitude. As a Supreme Being, there can be no question of God not accepting God's responsibilities.

A particular form of incarnation is, therefore, necessary, if God is supreme. God must genuinely experience what it is to live as a *moral human being*, with the same general level of knowledge, intelligence and aptitudes as other human beings. God must also experience a full range of human emotions, desires and limitations. Distinctively, however, God must experience suffering and the consequences of evil in a supreme way so that God does not consign humans to negative experiences that God is not prepared to face God-self; there would be something intrinsically wrong, if I could say that I have experienced greater suffering than God. Furthermore, God must do all of this in such a way that it can be known that this is how God has acted, enabling belief without coercing anyone into belief. This is the starting point for God accepting absolute responsibility for God's creative actions.

Is it comprehensible, however, to speak of God experiencing life as a human being? In other words, is the concept of incarnation a coherent one? If it is, then, if God exists, God will most certainly have become incarnate. If it is not a coherent concept, then God cannot have become incarnate. If God has not become incarnate, however, it seems to me that God has failed to act in a supremely good manner which implies that, in fact, God (understood as a Supreme Being) does not exist. The stakes really are quite high.

I suggested earlier, that a useful way of understanding God's interaction with human beings is to propose that while God is 'in' every human life, God does not direct how we think or act. As our minds emerge as a result of the sophisticated development of our brains, we are allowed a remarkable degree of autonomy. God is with us in all aspects of our lives and, as our minds are within

God's mind, it is possible for God to communicate with us without compromising our moral autonomy. God *could*, however, have chosen to act directly within and upon our emerging minds in such a way that all our thoughts are God's thoughts and all the perceptions mediated by our brains become God's perceptions. Such, I suggested did not happen, because human beings so constructed could not be distinguished in any meaningful way as autonomous individuals; they would be extensions, as it were, of God. If all human beings were like this, God would not, I concluded, have acted in a supremely creative way.

This does not mean, however, that *no* human being could be like this and I suggest that this is *one way* of understanding what is meant by incarnation: a Supreme Being expressing itself directly in a localised form in and as a human being. Such a concept is, I believe, a coherent one; one that enables God to experience precisely and exactly what it is to be a human being. Such a human, in effect with the mind of God encompassed in a genuinely human brain and body, would be no less than God-incarnate, the necessary prerequisite for God fully to accept the consequences of God's creation of semi-autonomous moral beings.

Living an Incarnate Life

Such an incarnation would not be at all obvious to anyone other than God. Even God-incarnate would not have a full knowledge of his or her 'identity' as, in order truly to experience the human condition, God would have to limit God's experience *as a human* only to those things that a human could know or understand; the life of God-incarnate would have to be a genuinely human life. To God-incarnate, life would be as it is for all humans: a mixture of knowledge and ignorance, joy and sorrow, pleasure and pain. It would be a life both of limitation and potential, marked by growing discernment, wisdom and understanding. God-incarnate could not know everything that there is to be known, but only that which he or she learned from human experience, intuition and reflection. Most certainly, God-incarnate would sense an affinity with God and, perhaps experience a growing conviction of unity with God, but this would fall short of any *knowledge* of incarnation. I find it fascinating to let my mind run riot around this idea; to try to grasp what it would be like for God to become truly incarnate. The thoughts, feelings, perceptions and experiences of God-incarnate would be genuinely human, but they would take place within a totally unique human being; another 'category of one'.

One area of the life of God-incarnate that is of particular theological significance and that demands my attention is that of 'sin', admittedly a rather unfashionable concept in many circles. Unfashionable or not, the topic must be addressed. If, from a theological perspective, I correctly interpret sin as neglect or rejection of God's will (inevitably resulting in harm being done to myself or to others), could it be possible that God-incarnate could sin? The answer that comes first to mind is that God-incarnate could not possibly reject God's will since the mind of God-incarnate is, essentially, the mind of God: God-incarnate could not, therefore, sin. This, seemingly, straightforward answer may, however, be misleading. If this were all that were to be said on the subject, it risks making incarnation something of a charade. How could God genuinely experience the human condition if God-incarnate did not face a real choice with regard to sin? Is *freedom* to choose to sin not an essential part of being a morally autonomous being?

It is true that not *all* human beings are morally autonomous. Small children and those with severe learning impairment, for example, are unable to make fully moral choices, but they are still, nonetheless, human persons. If God exists, I think that it is reasonable to suggest that such persons are still recipients of God's love and that their status as human beings are not diminished because of their lack of mental or moral development. The point of God acting in a supremely good and creative way in bringing into existence semi-autonomous moral beings is not that all humans *must* attain this status in order to enjoy God's love, but that this is the supreme moral 'end-point' of personal development that many human beings do, in fact, attain. Being able to choose whether or not to believe in God's existence and whether or not to respond positively to God is a high point in moral development. Those who are unable to make this choice are, I should like to think, no less human and no less valuable, but they either lack or have limited moral capacity. This does not make them any less recipients of God's love or worthy of human care. It seems to me unreasonable to suggest, however, that God-incarnate would lack moral capacity, thus allowing some humans to have a capacity that God-incarnate did not have. At the most fundamental level; therefore it must be the case that God-incarnate would have to make a genuine choice to believe in God and to obey God's will.

This presents me with a real conundrum. On the one hand, in order to be genuinely moral, God-incarnate must be able to make a genuine choice to accept or reject God's will, while on the other hand it would appear to be a nonsense to suggest that God-incarnate could possibly reject God's will without a fundamental and catastrophic rupturing of the very nature of God.

The conundrum does, however, have a solution. If viewed from a *transcendent* perspective, it is true that there could never be a possibility of God-incarnate sinning. God-incarnate and 'God-un-incarnate' are still God and the idea of a Supreme Being harbouring such a fundamental conflict is incoherent. Viewed in an *immanent* manner, however, the situation is quite different. Genuine incarnation would involve embracing all of humanity's limitations and weaknesses. This includes having access only to knowledge, perceptions, feelings and thoughts that can emerge from within human experience. As an incarnate being, God would face precisely the choices, temptations and moral dilemmas that all human beings face. As God-incarnate there could be no 'special pleading', relying on transcendent knowledge when making moral choices. If God were to become incarnate, as God must if God is a Supreme Being, then God's experience of being human would be precisely the same as that of every other human being, with the same real moral choices to be made. The fact that, when viewed from a different perspective I might conclude that God-incarnate would never make a wrong decision does not make the actual decision-making process any less real or less authentic for God-incarnate. The experience of being God–incarnate would be a fully human one in every sense, including the need to choose whether or not to obey God. Viewed from 'inside' the mind of God-incarnate, every decision is an authentic human one; viewed from 'outside', every decision is precisely that which only God would make if God were to become incarnate.

This means that were God to become incarnate, God would be immersed in the full range of human emotions and experiences, but that God-incarnate would do so in a manner that is in keeping with his or her own innate character. In every situation where a choice had to be made, the choice would be in accordance with God's will, but it would be a fully human decision, made after real and genuine thought, reflection and, at times, struggle. Temptation to make the wrong decision would be genuinely felt and all the weakness and limitations of being human would be present, but through this maze, decisions would emerge that would be in keeping with the mind of God.

Death

All of the above would enable God to enter fully into the experience of being human and this would mean that God could experience, *as a human being*, the full implications of God's creation of morally autonomous beings. Some of these implications would be positive: human love, laughter, companionship and creativity. Some, however, would be negative: human pain, suffering, loss and rejection.

Being human also means experiencing death in a particular way. As far as I am aware, of all creatures on Earth, only we humans are aware of our mortality and of the overwhelming loss of potential that death can represent. While it is essential in order for human evil to be limited, that we are not naturally eternal (imagine what the world would be like if all the despots and tyrants that ever lived were still around), death does, nonetheless, also represent a terrible loss of all that is good in a person's life. While it is true that we can invest ourselves in living lives that are positive in themselves and that our influence will continue for a while after we are gone, there is no doubt that death brings to an end both our actual and potential involvement in life on Earth.

In order for God-incarnate to experience the human condition in its fullness, it would be necessary for him or her to experience death; anything less would truly be a charade. Moreover, God-incarnate would have to face death with the same knowledge of mortality as all other human beings. In other words, while God-incarnate would, undoubtedly believe in God and perhaps also believe in some sort of life after death, he or she could not face death in the knowledge that *as God-incarnate*, death was for him or her nothing more than a minor interruption to life. Death might be faced with faith, but not with knowledge.

At the same time, it is, I suggest, unthinkable that God could allow the human life of God-incarnate to come to a complete end at death. The concept of God-incarnate *ceasing to exist* as God-incarnate is an extremely difficult one to comprehend. It is certainly much easier to think that God would not allow the life of God-incarnate to come to an end at death, but that God would ensure that God-incarnate would continue to exist, as a human being, beyond death.

This would be possible, if God were to 'preserve' the mind of God-incarnate, within the mind of God and then 'manifest' it in a new fashion; one that is more fully attuned to fulfilling and expressing all that the mind of God-incarnate truly is. If God is Fundamental Mind and mind is the essential 'stuff' of the universe, I cannot see any reason why the mind of God-incarnate could not be 'held' in the mind of God and, consequently 're-expressed', perhaps in a fashion that is 'hyper-physical' with real location and identity, but without many of the limitations imposed by matter/energy as we experience it. To borrow from Christian tradition, such an experience might correctly (if leadingly) be termed 'resurrection'. I have already noted that the universe is largely composed of dark matter and dark energy; who am I to say what configurations of mind might be possible? Equally, the mind of God-incarnate could continue to have personal identity within the mind of God, without having 'locality'; perhaps (to continue to utilise Christian terminology) representing a sort of 'spiritual resurrection'.

If God exists, I have outlined reasons for believing that God would become incarnate and experience all that humans must experience and that this would include death. If, as I have now suggested, God-incarnate would then be 're-expressed' or 'resurrected' rather than allowed to perish, God would then, in principle, have added something new and significant into the human condition. It also seems to me to be reasonable to suggest that if God were to be fair (as God surely would be), God would not introduce this new experience of resurrection as something that only God-incarnate would enjoy. If God did so, then God would not only display an unexpected degree of selfishness, but God would no longer really be participating in the fullness of the human experience since other humans do not experience resurrection. It is, therefore, a corollary of the resurrection of God-incarnate that other humans would also be resurrected by God. In effect, if God were to become incarnate, as God would surely do if God exists, God would be adding something new and distinctive to what it means to be human: the experience of being held as a person in the mind of God beyond death and being given a transformed existence in resurrection.

In other words, in choosing to create a universe in which semi-autonomous moral beings would emerge, God inevitably set in train a process that would see both good and evil, happiness and suffering also emerge. In order for God to be true to God's own character and nature, God would have to experience life *from within the universe*, as a moral being and this would entail suffering and death. Since extinction does not seem to be a likely outcome for the life of God-incarnate, resurrection also becomes an inevitable consequence of creation and, once more, in accordance with God's character and nature, resurrection would be something that God would extend to all human beings. None of this, of course, would come as a surprise to God, but would be understood to be part of the reality of God choosing to create a universe in which morally autonomous beings would emerge.

I think that I have gone some way in beginning to see how evil might be overcome by good, within the universe, but there is still some way to go before I am convinced that in creating the universe, God would, in fact, have done a good thing. That is the theme of my next chapter, but before I turn to it I want to acknowledge an alternative understanding of incarnation that I feel deserves attention.

Incarnation Re-visited

Earlier, I distinguished between what I called classical and dynamic theism and then introduced the concept of what I termed, *mystical* theism. This idea, I confess, stretches my mind to the full, particularly when I try to apply it to the subject of incarnation.

In mystical theism, it is, I think, possible to conceive of God becoming incarnate, not by living as a particular human being in the way outlined above, but by uniquely *absorbing* a particular human person into God's being, completely infusing that person with God's presence in such a way that it is henceforth impossible to speak of God without also speaking of that person or to speak of that person without also speaking of God. In this view of incarnation, God would unite with a particular human being in such a way that, within the limits of human experience, that human being would become God's very presence on earth and, in turn, would be encompassed by the limitless experience of God. Such an experience would go beyond the experience of even the most 'spiritual' and mystical of individuals. This would not be a case of a human surrendering his or her will to God; it would be complete and absolute personal unity: full inter-personal communion. Such a unity would rest on God's determination to unite fully with humanity and God's subsequent choice of an individual man or woman *and* on that particular human being's desire to be 'one' with God. I find it quite impossible to say what would constitute such purity of desire; a purity that would be genuinely devoid of self-interest or spiritual pride, though sometimes I think that I have a sense of what it might mean.

This understanding of the incarnation has the most profound implications for my understanding of God, because such an experience of absolute unity with a human being would also have to be understood as having eternal significance for God. Since

God is eternal, there is a sense in which the experience of incarnation would also be eternal: God and God's creation would be eternally united, making it impossible to think of one without the other. What that might mean for God is challenging enough for me to try to grasp; what it would mean for the human who became united with God, I cannot even begin to guess. *It would represent a fundamental choice by God to bring God's creation into God's very being.* As a result of one person's absolute unity with God, all of humanity would be radically altered. Human beings would become of infinite value and worth since, because of the experience of one human being, *humanity would lie at the very heart of God.* As such, the experience and destiny of one human being would result in a fundamental change in the experience of humanity; what it means to be human would include a destiny of union with God.

As I have said, such an understanding of the incarnation is essentially mystical in nature and defies description, never mind explanation, but I think that I can glimpse enough of it to recognise that it *could be* a viable way of understanding incarnation. I am not sure that I can entirely satisfy myself rationally, that such a 'process' would represent a true incarnation of God, although this might simply be a result of it being far removed from traditional Christian theology. Intuitively, however, I am unable to dismiss it. The important point, however, is that if God is a Supreme Being, God will choose to become incarnate; the means of God achieving this is a secondary matter and will certainly retain much mystery about it. In so far as this alternative understanding of incarnation *might* represent insight into a true incarnation, it remains something that, I believe, could reflect reality. This experience of God-incarnate would, of course, encompass temptation, suffering, death and resurrection in much the same way as outlined in the earlier understanding of incarnation, but my appreciation of those experiences might also, perhaps, be grasped more intuitively than rationally. Sinlessness, for example could be understood as something that emanated from union with God, not something that necessarily existed prior to that essential union taking place. There is, I believe, much room here for thought and reflection.

In the rest of this book, when I speak of incarnation, I shall mostly have the earlier theory in mind, but I shall reflect also on this latter theory, allowing its challenges to inform and colour my thinking without actively advocating it.

Chapter Eleven

Love Wins – Overcoming Evil
(The Necessity of Death… The Question of Punishment…
The Power of Love)

If I am correct in suggesting that by becoming incarnate and experiencing suffering, death and resurrection, God has ensured that experiencing resurrection is part of what it means to be human, then at one level, at least, it might be argued that evil *has* been overcome. While human suffering can be extreme, it is unlikely that even those who have suffered most would not accept that their suffering has been compensated by their experience of resurrection, if that experience is *both permanent and positive*. These caveats are, however, necessary. Almost any degree of limited suffering or pain would be worthwhile if it was followed by an unlimited, positive experience of life, in particular, a 'higher' expression of life that would forever be free from further pain or distress. Resurrection, after death, would provide 'restitution', as it were, for all of the ills, however great, suffered prior to death. Is however, such an expression of life possible? Does it make sense to think that an experience of resurrection could be permanent, and if it is, how could such an experience also be positive?

In looking at the possibility of resurrection being both permanent and positive, I think that is it important to look, first of all, at reasons why human life at present is non-permanent, coming to an end with death. While it is natural for humans to view death as 'the final enemy', this is only so if it is viewed in the absence of the possibility of resurrection. If, however, resurrection is admitted as a possibility, then death takes on a very different role. Instead of representing an end to all that is good in human life and experience, it may be viewed as placing a limitation on evil as well as providing a gateway for life to fulfil its potential. In other words, 'physical' human life is not permanent because it is not *sufficiently* positive.

I have already suggested that it would be a terrible thing if various despots in history were to still be alive today; the pain and suffering that they would cause would be literally, limitless. Similarly, though at a lesser level, all humans inflict some degree of suffering on others. Indeed, the sorry history of the human race indicates that we are much better at harming one another than we are at loving one another. Even within our closest and best relationships, hurt and pain are never far from the surface. In an environment where God's existence will always be contested, there is nothing to suggest that human beings would ever get any better at living better lives. Throughout history, atrocities have occurred in sophisticated as well as in primitive societies, intrigue and violence have been prevalent among cultured as well as among ignorant individuals and many men and women have demonstrated devotion and compassion to their families, but have been known to act with chilling cruelty to others. If 'natural' human lives were endless, so too would suffering and pain.

Equally, if 'natural' human lives were to extend forever, they would very soon lose their sparkle and enjoyment. Much as I love football, I think that an *endless* succession of world cups would, eventually, hold no attraction for me. I am not sure how even the best of relationships would survive if they stayed at essentially the same level forever and I think that even the most creative people would find that their creativity would dry up once it hit an inevitable plateau: just how many symphonies would Mozart complete if he had billions of years at his disposal?. It has been reported that Winston Churchill's last words before he lapsed into a coma before his death were 'I'm bored by it all'. This, I think, would be the universal human experience if life were simply more and more of the same.

Of course, if humans were naturally immortal, I and the rest of my generation would never have been born; the planet would have reached its population capacity hundreds, if not thousands, of years ago and the human race would have been forced to stop propagating; a challenging thought in itself. All in all, within the confines of earthly existence, death is very much a 'necessary evil'.

How then might resurrection be any different? Certainly, if by resurrection, I were to mean 'more of the same', it would not, and the prospect could not be a positive one. There are, however, a number of factors that, if seen as being intrinsic to the experience of resurrection, have the capacity to transform human life. The first, and most important, is that, *if God exists*, resurrection, whether understood as a 'hyper-physical' or 'spiritual' experience, could include direct and certain communication with God. As I have already suggested, such certainty of God's existence and knowledge of God's character would have an overwhelming influence on how I choose to live. If to these factors, I were to add, direct communication with God and an exponentially expanding relationship with God, then I believe that all possibility of my choosing to act in a harmful or negative way would be extinguished. Just as I am personally unable to think or to act negatively while I am cheering a winning goal or, conversely, while savouring a moment of tranquillity, I cannot see how I could possibly think and act other than in a wholly positive way 'in the presence' of God. The impact of being with a Supreme Being, would I think, be supremely glorious. As there is no reason to believe that such an experience would, subsequently, be withdrawn by God, a resurrected life would truly be a transformed life.

In contrast to life being 'more of the same', resurrected life could be 'more of more'; an unending experience of growth, with my mind, my experiences and my creativity expanding eternally. By bringing resurrection into the human experience, God has transformed what it means to be human and has, in the process, rendered limited experiences of pain or suffering, however terrible, worthwhile steps on the road to truly fulfilled lives.

The Price of Morality

There is still, however, a further problem to be addressed, before I can be assured that God has acted morally in creating a universe containing morally autonomous beings: the problem of personal culpability for wrong-doing. The core of the problem is that, even though the evil that we humans perpetrate might be limited, it is nonetheless, real and cannot simply be ignored. I do not think that it is *sufficient* to say that evil is the price we pay for moral autonomy and that God 'covers' the consequences of this by making resurrection part of human experience. This may demonstrate God's moral character in facing God's responsibilities as creator, but it does not address the issue of *our* moral responsibilities as creatures.

I have an innate sense that it would be morally wrong if the hurt and pain that I have caused others, and that others have caused me, were to be brushed under the carpet. No matter how kind, loving or compassionate God might be, I cannot see that it would be right for God simply to act as if none of this really mattered. While, in some sense, sin may be regarded as a type of moral sickness causing humans to act in selfish ways, again, it is not *sufficient* to treat it in this way. Even though I know that I cannot avoid the inevitability of committing some sins during my life, I am morally responsible for choosing which particular sins I commit. From my childhood choice to allow another child to take the blame for my clumsiness in failing to catch a ball, all the way through to the crimes of mass-murderers, it would be morally wrong if such actions were to be ignored or condoned.

There is, I think, a problem that many (though by no means, all) people living in relative comfort in economically developed countries face, that makes it difficult for them to appreciate the true horror of sin. The problem is that their worst experience of sin is likely to be relatively minor: a row at home, a personal slight at work or similar relational problems. I do not want to minimise the impact of such experiences, but I also think that it is essential that I point out that the reality of sin for very many people is so much greater than this. People being trafficked into sex-slavery, labourers being forced to work for a pittance, often in appalling conditions, domestic violence, rape, grinding poverty and murder form the backdrop to millions upon millions of people's lives.

I have an avid interest in history; I simply love reading about it, studying it, thinking about it and discussing it with anyone who is prepared to listen. One thing that stands out to me throughout human history is that, for the greater part, it has been marked by the most terrible suffering inflicted by humans upon one another. Much as I should like to find human achievements in art, music, literature, science and medicine the focus of human history I would be deluding myself to think that such is the case. Very slowly, over millennia, we have struggled to achieve greater degrees of 'civilisation', but the cost must be counted in hundreds of millions of shattered lives. Even now, in the relative comfort and security of the economically developed world, I often think that only a thin veil separates us from descending into moral and social chaos.

I have a personal pact with my own conscience that states that every few months I must read accounts of slavery, watch footage of atrocities such as the Holocaust and delve into the shocking and seedy reality of the effects of human power, greed and selfishness. I do so, not because I enjoy the experience, but I know that all too easily I can dismiss the reality of human sin to the level of some personal affront that I have experienced. Unless I am regularly confronted by images of Auschwitz, of the reality of war and of the sheer corruption and evil of human trafficking, I am prone to minimise the reality of sin. I confess that I struggle with the attitude of many people when they say that they will not face such reality because they find it too upsetting. 'Be upset', I want to tell them, 'and then perhaps you will want to do something about it'. People pay the price for sin every second of every day; the least that I can do is face the reality of it.

Human legal systems attempt to introduce some degree of moral appreciation of wrong-doing through the administration of punishment and the requirements of restitution. While these go some way in emphasising the seriousness of wrong-doing, they do not, of course, adequately address the moral implications of sin. They represent essentially external 'remedies' to actions that have both an external and an internal dimension. The external dimension is the hurt inflicted on victims; the internal dimension is the culpability, guilt and moral failings of perpetrators. I have suggested that, at a theological level, the external dimension of sin may be dealt with through the experience of resurrection providing restitution for temporal suffering. The restitution is not provided by the perpetrator, but by God, who assumes responsibility for the actions of God's creatures. This is, of course, the only way in which restitution could possibly be made: how could I ever provide restitution to all the people that I have hurt or treated badly throughout the course of my life? Such restitution would be an act of supreme goodness on God's part, reflecting the nature and the character of God.

If restitution addresses the external problem of sin, I suggest that punishment, *properly understood*, might enable me to find a solution for the internal problem of sin. The point of punishment, it seems to me, is not to cause gratuitous pain or suffering or to 'get even', but to try to impress personally upon the perpetrator of a crime, the true nature of his or her actions. One way of making me realise the enormity of my actions is for me to experience punishment: a degree of pain, loss or discomfort that reflects the degree of pain, loss or discomfort that I have caused another person to experience. This, in human hands, is very much a 'hit or miss' affair; we can seldom agree what an appropriate punishment ought to be for a particular crime, but we still have some shared sense that crime ought not to go unpunished. Again, while in human hands, punishment is often, wrongly, associated with a desire for revenge, the principle is still clear: punishment has the potential to bring wrong-doers to their senses by enabling them to appreciate as fully as possible, the nature and extent of the wrong they have caused. Within human criminal justice systems, once offenders recognise the wrong they have done and are not thought to represent a danger to others, they are often admitted back into society.

Of course, wrong-doing includes much more than criminal offences. All hurts, inflicted on others, are morally wrong, whether they are inflicted directly or indirectly. In some cases, even hurts inflicted unintentionally may be morally wrong if they are the results or carelessness or neglect. For this reason, while we might not seek a legal remedy for each offence we suffer, we often withhold or withdraw our affection or company from those who have hurt us. We might not always be conscious of it, but one reason for acting in this way is to enable those who have wronged us to realise the enormity of what they have done.

How though, could I ever realise the full implications of all my actions? How could I possibly ever really appreciate the harm and pain that I have caused others? The answer seems to be that it would literally take me all of eternity truly to appreciate what I have done and as long again (if such a thing were possible) to stop feeling remorse for my actions. This is true if I were to think only of the pain and hurt that I have caused other human beings; it is even more so if I think of the pain that I have caused God, should God exist. To be left eternally alone, to consider and to appreciate my wrong-doing, having my eyes opened to what I had done, would truly be what I would deserve. If this were to happen, however, resurrection would never enable God to overcome evil; it would simply enable God to extend my life so that I could come to appreciate the wrong that I had done. Resurrection would, in fact, become a doorway, not to eternal life, but to eternal punishment.

There is, I am glad to say, another way in which God could enable me to 'come to my senses'. Instead of being overcome by punishment, I could be overcome by love. When I wrong someone, I know, from my own experience, that if he or she responds, not in anger, but in love, I appreciate not only the true nature of my actions but also the liberating and cleansing effects of forgiveness. If, in the resurrection, God meets me, not with punishment, but with love, the possibility exists for me both to appreciate the wrong that I have done and to have that experience transformed into something that is truly life-enhancing. *This cannot be a trivial matter*; I should need to recognise the depth of love that God is demonstrating in choosing to offer me this prospect rather than requiring me to face my past alone. The love that is typified by God's willingness to take responsibility for enabling me to be a morally autonomous being, by becoming incarnate and by undergoing suffering and death so that my rehabilitation can be effected, is such a love.

Of course, my wrong-doing will not just affect God; it will also affect others. Is it right, therefore, even if God wishes to respond to my sin with love, that God can do so without the agreement of others whom I have wronged? I think that this would present a problem if any of the people I have hurt were, themselves, blameless. I know, however, that such is not the case; we are all both victims and perpetrators. By assuming moral responsibility for the actions of all human beings, God has, I think the moral right to determine whether or not I and others ought to be treated with love or with punishment. The fact that God chooses to respond with love, bears testament to God's character and nature.

There is, however, one caveat to this. It is not inevitable that I or others will respond to love by seeing this as a means of 'coming to our senses' and being rehabilitated. I can always reject the full implications of love and refuse to allow love to work fully on my heart and mind. In effect, I can reject love and choose, instead, to cling to my own selfishness. In such circumstances, I think that God must then allow me to reject God's love and allow me to be left to my own devices. My fate would then be to experience the punishment of being without God's love while being presented with the reality of my actions. This would, however, be my choice. Love can never be coercive; however I might experience the offer of God's love in the resurrection, it must not undermine my status as a moral being. I think that it is reasonable to suggest that if I have been open to the love of God (*knowingly or not*) before I die, I shall be open to the love of God in the resurrection and if I have been closed to the love of God before I die, I might still be closed to God's love in the resurrection. My 'choice' is likely to be the response of my essential moral orientation (fashioned throughout my life), rather than as a result of rational decision. Such is the love of God, of course, that it is entirely possible that it will continue to pursue even the most recalcitrant of hearts into the resurrection and beyond.

What all of this means is that God is able to overcome evil by making resurrection a part of the human experience and by offering forgiveness to all who choose to accept God's love. As all morally autonomous humans are both perpetrators and victims, we are all given the 'gift' of resurrection and we are all given the choice of accepting God's love. Even though all might not accept the love of God, I suggest that God can ethically make a universe in which morally autonomous being emerge, because in taking full responsibility for God's actions, God has made full restitution to all who have suffered and offered a full and perfect life to all who wish to accept it.

Chapter Twelve

Christian Theology – A Brief Outline

(Creation… Trinity… Incarnation… Salvation… Revelation…
Christian Living… Prayer)

What I have outlined so far in my examination of what God might
be like (should God exist) has not been specifically referenced to
the Christian Faith. Nonetheless, it is obvious that what I have
been outlining has marked similarities with a Christian
understanding of God. To what extent this is the case because I
have been influenced by my prior knowledge of Christianity to
think in a certain way, and to what extent it is the case because
Christianity explores many of the issues that I believe it is important
to explore, is open to debate. I am not sure that it really matters,
however, since I am convinced both that a believable understanding
of God must include the topics that I have covered and that these
topics are covered in Christianity.

As I observed in my opening chapter, even though there are many
varieties of Christianity, I do not intend to explore them all. That
would, no doubt, be fascinating, but it is not necessary for me to
delve into the labyrinthine world of confessional theology in order
to pursue my own quest. At this stage of my enquiry I am interested
in trying to find an understanding of Christianity that is, *to me*,
both reasonable and defensible. This might seem to be a very self-
centred approach to take to one of the world's great religions, but
this book is an account of a journey of exploration; not a critique,
or a defence, of the Christian religion. For this reason, as I outlined
earlier, I have chosen to italicise the word *Christian*, to refer to *my*
views.

I believe, as Christianity clearly covers many of the topics that I have covered, that it is reasonable to see if my theology is compatible with a form of Christianity. To put it differently: I want now to explore what, in my opinion, a believable and defensible basic *Christian* theology might look like. *This, of course, does not imply that such a theology is true or that alternative theologies or philosophies are false.* As I write about it in this section of the book, however, I shall write *as if it were true*; to do otherwise would necessitate a tedious repetition of disclaimers. To be clear: I am exploring the *coherence* or otherwise of a *Christian* understanding of God; whether there are grounds for believing that such an understanding is true, I shall leave to the final section of this book.

Creation

As I commented earlier, I do not believe that there is any conflict between science and theology as far as understanding the existence of the universe is concerned, unless I am tempted to retreat into either materialist or creationist fundamentalism, and, happily for me, I am not. The concept of God being 'behind' and 'within' the creation and the development of the universe may be understood in ways that are in keeping with our best scientific understanding and vice-versa. Of course, just as scientists know only a fraction of what there is to be known in the universe, I cannot be sure that the best that science offers does, in fact, correspond to reality in every instance. Nonetheless, with this important caveat noted, I can see no reason why God could not or should not have created both the universe and the scientific and mathematical laws that gave rise to it and that sustain it. To say that God *did* so would be, of course, not a matter of certainty, but of faith and in the final section of this book I shall examine whether or not such faith might be justified. In principle, however, there is nothing incoherent or illogical about it.

This is in keeping with the teaching of the Christian Scriptures where belief in God's creation of the world is openly presented as a faith issue; there is, therefore no need for me to try to *prove* that God created the universe in order to suggest that a *Christian* theology might be correct. Indeed, as I have already argued, any such proof would be counter-productive as it would compromise human beings' freedom to make a moral choice with regard to belief in God which would, consequently, undermine the genuinely moral nature of the human race.

Perhaps my suggestion that God created the universe as an expression of God-self, rather than as something wholly 'other' than God-self, may be controversial for some Christians. While this might be so, I cannot see that such a theory is in any way contrary to *Christian* belief and for the reasons that I have already outlined, it seems to me to be both a more appealing and more coherent theory than that usually promoted within classical theism. Others, of course, are free to disagree and to propose other theories.

A *Christian* understanding of creation proposes that the universe has meaning; that it has been created for a purpose. Initially, that purpose is to enable the emergence of semi-autonomous, creative beings that are able to relate not only to one another but to the rest of the universe and, *most importantly to God*, in a moral manner. From my perspective, that means that I am able to make genuinely moral decisions with regard to how I live my life, how I treat other people, how I engage with the environment and whether or not I choose to believe in and follow God. If true, this makes me and other human beings, immeasurably 'valuable'. Simply because I often take who and what I am for granted, does not mean that I should become unappreciative of the astounding fact that I and other similar beings have come into existence. It may well be the case that it requires an entire universe or even multiverse to produce human or other similar beings just as it takes billions of human beings to produce a Shakespeare or a Mozart; this suggests that, should God exist, God values human life very highly indeed.

The purpose in God creating the universe is not, however, exhausted by the emergence of semi-autonomous moral beings. This is, in fact, only the first step; the final purpose is to see human beings (and perhaps others) enter into a positive relationship with God which results in them enjoying an expression of life that is as full and as creative as possible. The universe is, in fact, the prequel to the main performance. I shall return to this thought presently, in the section on 'salvation'.

Trinity

The doctrine of the Trinity is unique to Christianity; so too, is belief in a single, 'communal' Supreme Being. I confess that I find this a little strange as it seems to me that for a Supreme Being to be supreme it must have relationship within itself. I acknowledge that *some* forms of Hinduism and other 'Eastern' religions embrace this viewpoint, but it is not a belief that is held at a popular level other than within Christianity. Truth to be told, however, my experience suggests that most Christians are not really Trinitarians, but tri-theists using Trinitarian language. Perhaps the concept of a single 'communal' being' *is* difficult to embrace. Difficult or not, it (or something even more intellectually demanding as outlined earlier in *mystical theism*) is, I believe, essential if God is to be understood as a Supreme Being.

There is little evidence within the Christian Scriptures that belief in Trinity came about through the sort of philosophical and theological reflections discussed in this book. It seems to have emerged, initially at least, as a means of interpreting the experience of the first Christians who came to believe that Jesus was 'one with

God' while they also continued to adhere to the belief that God was one. Their further experiences of what they considered to be the continuing presence of Jesus also led them to believe in the divinity of the Holy Spirit and so the ground was laid for the development of a Trinitarian *theodigm*. Again, I shall examine whether or not such belief is credible in the final section of this book, but for the moment, my concern is to see how this fits into the *theodigm* of God that I have already suggested.

In positing a single, communal personality for God, it might be argued that, in theory, God could have any number of 'personal centres', rather than the three proposed by Christian faith. It might equally be argued that while the Christian Faith states that God exists in and as three 'persons', this does not necessarily mean that other 'persons' could not exist although they have not been revealed to the human race. Both of these statements might be true, but there are reasons for believing that if God is a single, communal being, there are most likely three, and only three, 'personal centres' within God.

The reason for there being two 'personal centres' is obvious: the need to ensure relationship as something intrinsic to God, whether that relationship is based on God's eternal, intrinsic *being* or on God's eternal, intrinsic *creativity*. Less obvious, but just as essential, however, is the need for relationship to be non-exclusive. An exclusive relationship lacks something and that something is an experience of community in which the good of *all* is sought as a supreme good. Two may be enough for relationship, but three is required for community. A communal relationship is richer than an exclusive, dual relationship and it is, I think, reasonable to suggest that God's intrinsic relationships would be rich. There is, however, no need for more than three 'persons' to give an authentic experience of community and as God is a self-existent and self-ordered being, I cannot see why God would choose to have more than three personal centres. Indeed, it is possible to view the existence of more than three personal centres in God as a selfish act in which God's creativity would be unnecessarily 'internally' focused rather than 'externally' focused in the creation of new, 'other' beings.

A *Christian* view of Trinity might, therefore be understood as a single self-existent being *necessarily* existing as an utterly unified personal community with three identifiable 'personal centres'. In the Christian tradition the name given to this being is God and the names given to the 'personal centres' are Father, Son and Holy Spirit. Because each 'personal centre' is entirely one with the others and each enjoys the same divine nature, it is also possible to call each of them 'God' since they never exist other than together; in perfect knowledge and relationship. Such, I believe is a defensible *Christian* understanding of God. As I stated earlier, continued reflection on mystical theism might also open up new avenues of exploration that could enable a refinement of Trinitarian belief, so, for me at least, this remains unfinished business. I am intrigued by such a thought, indicating that when I complete this enquiry there will still be much more to explore. In truth, if God exists, I suspect that the journey of exploration will be never-ending; a mouth-watering prospect.

Incarnation

I have argued that, if God is a Supreme Being, then God will be supremely moral and will take full responsibility for creating a universe in which semi-autonomous moral beings will emerge. This responsibility will include the necessity of incarnation.

Within the Christian Faith, Jesus is seen as being God-incarnate, although it has to be said that the full implications of this statement are often masked by frequent references in Christian literature to Jesus as the 'Son of God'. While this is a way of enabling Christians to identify Jesus with the 'second person of the Trinity' in distinction from the 'Father' and the 'Holy Spirit', it seems it me often to have the unfortunate effect of suggesting that Jesus was not God-incarnate, but some sort of demigod. In the early development of Christian theology, some groups such as the Arians did, in fact, argue that this was the case: Jesus was a special creation of God known, pre-incarnation as the Logos and post-incarnation as Jesus of Nazareth with the risen Jesus most often referred to as 'the Christ'. From time to time, within the history of Christianity, various groups have emerged that have adopted this doctrine: I also suspect that this is what many 'ordinary' Christians believe.

I have already outlined the importance of God becoming incarnate as a necessary corollary of God, as a Supreme Being, acting in a supremely moral manner. If the Logos was, however, not God, but a special creation placed somewhere between God and the human race, then the incarnation of the Logos would fail entirely to address the need for God to become incarnate. The 'traditional' Christian doctrine of Jesus being God-incarnate is, I think, not only correct, but necessary. *If* God exists, then a belief in Jesus as God-incarnate is a coherent one; belief in Jesus as an incarnation of a demigod lacks coherence entirely.

An understanding of incarnation in which Jesus, the man, was united fully with God and 'absorbed' into God's presence and 'infused' completely by it, is certainly not part of a traditional understanding of the incarnation. *If*, however, it can be understood as effecting a real incarnation, it seems to me that it could represent an authentic Christian viewpoint. *If God exists*, I am currently inclined to think that an understanding of the incarnation that reflects *dynamic* theism is likely to be closer to the truth than an understanding of the incarnation based on what I have termed *mystical* theism. Nonetheless, I am not prepared to dismiss it unless it can be shown that mystical theism *could not* effect a true incarnation; I am not convinced that such is the case.

However, I might view the *means* by which the incarnation could be effected, the essential life-story of Jesus would appear to meet all the criteria that I outlined earlier with regard to God becoming incarnate. Jesus certainly seems to have lived a genuinely human life, subject to human limitations. He is recorded as enduring physical and psychological hardship, suffering and pain as well as enjoying human comforts, food, drink and close friendships. His death, in particular, encapsulated much of 'the human experience': love, betrayal, injustice, suffering, humiliation, nobility, courage and endurance. The accounts of his resurrection are also in keeping with my suggestion that if God were to become incarnate, not only must God-incarnate experience death, but that his or her death could not be the end of the story. I am not, thereby, saying that the accounts of the resurrection of Jesus are true, but that *if they are*, they are in keeping with what I should expect from an account of the life of God-incarnate.

Salvation

It is difficult to talk of the incarnation without also examining the topic of salvation: the purpose behind the incarnation. Salvation, in the Christian tradition, includes such experiences as a definitive response to sin, forgiveness, new life and resurrection. While I have outlined earlier how all of these flow from God's character and God's decision to create semi-autonomous moral beings, I think that it is useful to look at them again in the context of proposing a *Christian* theology of salvation.

If the end purpose of creation is to enable an array of semi-autonomous moral beings to enjoy participation in the sort of creative life that God enjoys, then this, it seems to me, is a very good thing for God to have done. It does not come, however, without serious attendant difficulties which include much distress, pain and suffering for many people as well as for other creatures. The end goal *and the means of attaining it*, must, therefore, be such that all the negative corollaries of creation can be clearly seen as being both necessary and worthwhile.

I have outlined how a *Christian* understanding of creation and incarnation addresses the need for God to take seriously God's responsibilities in choosing to create morally autonomous moral beings. I also argued earlier, that if God is to overcome evil and suffering, then God must not only experience this for God-self, but that God must also make that experience part of a greater experience of life in which pain, suffering and evil are 'absorbed' and transformed. This, I suggested could happen by God-incarnate experiencing death and resurrection. The common human experience of pain, suffering and evil may then be addressed fully by resurrection becoming part of the human experience. Our *current experience* of creation, therefore, becomes a necessary stepping stone to a *fuller experience* of creation. Such, an experience, however, while it must be offered to all, cannot be imposed on anyone, in order that our status as moral beings is not compromised. A free choice to accept or to reject a 'full' life, in which personal experience of both inflicting and enduring suffering is reconciled, is possible through an experience of the love of God. The choice to accept or to reject is, however, a real one and those who choose to reject this path cannot morally object to the consequences of their decision.

All of this, it seems to me, is compatible with the Christian tradition, although, of course, such a *Christian* understanding of salvation will not be universally accepted by all Christians. Nonetheless, I shall attempt to outline further a *Christian* understanding of it.

It is probably necessary to begin rather negatively by looking at 'sin'. If sin is understood as everything and anything that is not in keeping with God's way of thinking and acting, then clearly, we human beings have a sin problem. I have already outlined reasons why, as semi-autonomous moral beings, we cannot be coerced into having either certain knowledge of God or of God's way of doing things. The problem is, therefore, partly inherent: how *could* we always know and, subsequently, choose to think and act as God would? It is, however, also *partly deliberate*: even when we believe that we do know how we ought to act, we often choose not to. The effects of sin are far-reaching, covering everything from personal insult to genocide, and cannot morally be ignored either by God or by us.

If Jesus is seen as being God-incarnate, then God has entered fully into the human experience and has endured all that humans endure. Jesus' trial and subsequent death by crucifixion, a very cruel and painful form of execution, demonstrate that in him, God has embraced the consequences of choosing to create human beings. In the resurrection of Jesus from the dead, God has also demonstrated that sin, evil and suffering do not have the final say in the universe, but that they have been absorbed and overcome by the essential goodness of God. The experience of resurrection is, therefore, extended to all.

There have been many theories of *atonement* proposed during the history of Christianity, most of them employing metaphors to try to make their point. Referring back to my earlier illustration of Bohr's diagram of the atom, it is possible to view most of these as pointing towards some aspects of the actual reality of salvation. They each employ their own *theodigm* and they each seek to cast light on something that, because it emanates from God, can never be fully understood. I am not going to comment on these various theories other than to say that in so far as they indicate that salvation is something that is entirely God-based, coming from the nature and character of God and that it is not in any way based on God demanding human beings to make amends for their wrongdoing (an impossible task), they add something to my understanding of salvation. Where they become ever more intricate and demanding of their adherents, being presented as the *only* way of understanding salvation, I tend to part company with them.

I think that it is reasonable to say that the death of Jesus on the cross principally demonstrates God's *love* for the human race. It is the supreme example of a Supreme Being, God, taking upon God-self all of the consequences of creation, refusing to abandon humans to their lot. The resurrection is, then, the means by which God removes the necessity of any human being facing personal condemnation for the sins that he or she has committed. For this reason, the death and resurrection of Jesus are inseparable companions in *Christian* theology.

I think that it is right, therefore, to stress that Jesus *suffered* for the sins of humanity, rather than that he was *punished* for them, other than in the sense that some of his contemporaries tortured and killed him as a punishment for what they considered to be serious crimes (blasphemy for the Jerusalem authorities; treason for the Romans). The biblical concept of the 'wrath of God' is best presented as an unchanging opposition to wrong-doing accompanied by the need for wrong-doers to realise the enormity of their actions, rather than as anything that could possibly indicate a vindictive pleasure in inflicting punishment. The idea of God being vindictive or needing to be appeased or placated is a common misunderstanding of God's nature and character and of God's relationship with humans, which has been present throughout human history. This view of God, it is true, also forms a backcloth to some of the Christian scriptures' treatment of atonement. This is understandable as it was necessary for the first Christian evangelists and apologists to address the concerns that people had;

not the concerns that they ought to have had. Therefore, while there are parts of the New Testament that do speak in terms of God's 'wrath' being turned away, I believe that they are best read in the context of God assuming responsibility for creation and, in so doing, removing all need for judgement. Jesus' picture of God as a father who forgives the most errant of offspring and the New Testament statement, 'God is love', suggest very strongly that any understanding of atonement must begin and end with that aspect of God's character.

That a need for judgement would exist, in the absence of the suffering, death and resurrection of God-incarnate, seems to me to be evident if we are to be considered as moral beings. As I have stated earlier, it is not enough to view sin as a sickness; it ought also to be viewed as an evil. A *Christian* theology of forgiveness and judgement indicates that the requirement for all of us to realise the extent of our wrong-doing can be met if we embrace the extent of God's love for us, in relationship with God who 'is love'. As we experience the love of God, we will also come to appreciate the true awfulness of our sin; awfulness so great that it required God-self to experience it in order to set us free from its grasp. A *Christian* theology of salvation will, therefore embrace Jesus, as effecting the means by which humans may be reconciled to God. As God-Incarnate, Jesus alone has transformed the very nature and future of humanity through the incarnation, the cross and the resurrection.

It is not, of course, necessary for individuals to have a correct theology, or even to know anything about theology at all, in order to 'choose God'. Such a choice is, I believe, indicated by a basic orientation, freely chosen, to be open to the God of love and, consequently, to love's requirements. It is not possible for everyone in the world to hear about the Christian or any other faith, but love is a universal phenomenon that mediates God's character and presence. If the phrase, 'God is love' means anything, it must, at least mean this. I have deliberately tried to keep biblical quotations to a minimum in this book since it is an examination of theology, not a Bible-study. Such is the importance, however, of understanding that God *is* love and that by 'choosing' love we are choosing God, that it is helpful for me to take note of a mature reflection contained in one of the later documents found in the New Testament: '*Beloved, let us love one another, for love is from God, and* **whoever loves has been born of God and knows God***. Anyone who does not love does not know God, because God is love*' (1 John 4: 7, 8 my emphasis).

In this way, it is possible for people with varying *theodigms*, or with none at all, to respond positively to God. It is even possible for individuals to respond very negatively to *theodigms* that they believe indicate what God is like and still to respond positively to God. Similarly, it is possible for individuals to adhere to *theodigms* that might well represent God with a good degree of accuracy, but nonetheless, fail to embrace the essential character and nature of God. Embracing love will, I believe, eventually lead to individuals realising that they have, in fact, embraced God, while refusing to embrace love will mean that individuals will realise that they have failed to embrace God. Embracing God, will enable us to realise the extent of our wrong-doing as we experience the greatness of God's love demonstrated in the life, death and resurrection of Jesus. Refusing to embrace God will cause us to feel the unmitigated effects of God's opposition to wrong-doing without the all-important, transforming 'filter' of God's love.

Heaven and hell might, therefore, both be seen as an experience of the presence of God; one, an experience of love because we have embraced love; the other an experience of loss because we have failed to embrace love. The picture of God being 'light' is a common one in the Christian Scriptures. Our encounter with the 'light' can either be a warming and illuminating experience or it can be a blinding, searing one. I propose that a *Christian* understanding of salvation suggests that the choice is ours.

How then might humans experience salvation? Most certainly, not by trying to appease God or by trying to claim that our good deeds outweigh our bad ones. I have already indicated that such moral arithmetic is nonsense. The common Christian teaching is that salvation comes to us as a gift from God and this is often termed, 'grace'. I suggest that not only is this correct, but that 'grace' ought to be seen as extending to everything that God gives us, including the gift of life itself. Equally prominent in Christian teaching is that humans ought to respond to God by 'faith', if we are to receive God's grace. I believe that this means that if we are to receive God's love we must respond by saying 'yes' to God, which, in effect, is saying 'yes' to love. Faith is, therefore, not so much a 'mind-set' as a 'heart-set'. This is entirely in keeping with the important principle, mentioned earlier, that if God exists, God will be accessible to people with varying intellectual capacities.

Does this mean, however, that faith has no intellectual content? I do not believe so. If God is love, then it is important to *understand* as well as to experience all that love is: all that God is. A misunderstanding of the nature of God has led the human race to embrace truly crazy activities in attempts to appease God and to engage in truly horrendous activities in attempts to coerce others into belief. To know about God and God's character and nature is, therefore, of the utmost importance. The question might reasonably be asked, therefore, how might we know what is true?

Revelation

I have already argued that, *if God exists* and has created the universe so that semi-autonomous moral beings will emerge within it, it is almost certain that God will wish to communicate with such beings. I have also suggested that the *end-goal* of creation is not that semi-autonomous moral creatures will emerge within the universe, but that these creatures might have the opportunity of continuing to live 'with' God in a transformed state; one that is impervious to the change and decay evident in our current experience. If this is so, it is necessary for God to communicate with human beings; without communication there is no possibility of a meaningful relationship. While communication does not always have to be either verbally or intellectually grasped, it will, at times, include such forms of communication for those for whom it is appropriate. In other words, I should expect God to communicate to human beings something about God's nature, character and purposes so that people might be able to make an informed choice with regard to believing in God's existence. While I believe that, if God exists, God may be described as being 'love', it is necessary for 'love' to be given real content so that I and others might understand better how to respond and to relate to it.

How might God achieve this, without compromising the moral autonomy of human beings, in other words, without overstepping the mark and making God's presence a provable fact? I have already suggested that God ought to be able to interact with human minds in a subtle way, possibly through the ways in which the right and left hemispheres of our brains combine to enable our minds to reflect on the moral and spiritual significance of life. As we share our experiences and thoughts with one another, varying degrees of consensus among individuals will assist the growth of communal philosophies and religions. Even though the results of communal reflection will vary, *if God exists*, I should expect that many people will come to recognise that such things as love, honesty and compassion are good things while such things as violence, greed and selfishness are bad things. In a generalised sense, the very existence of the universe, the nature of human relationships and individual personal reflection can all be vehicles for God's revelation.

The Christian tradition, however, claims that God's self revelation to the human race goes far beyond God influencing this general moral and spiritual sense that all humans experience. Other religions, of course, make similar claims, but, for the reasons I outlined earlier, in this study I am exploring the claims of Christianity.

Christians claim that God has revealed God-self ultimately as God-incarnate in the person of Jesus of Nazareth. In order to prepare human beings for the incarnation, Christians also claim that God specifically revealed particular aspects of God's nature and character in and through the history of the Jewish people. This does not imply that God did not reveal *anything* of God-self to other groups. Without such a protracted period of preparation, however, while the incarnation would still have accomplished all that God intended it to, its meaning would have remained largely inaccessible. Christians further claim, that after the resurrection of Jesus, guided by the Holy Spirit, his early followers reflected on the significance of his death and life, coming to an appreciation of his role in effecting human salvation. Chosen accounts of God's preparatory revelation, of the life, death and resurrection of Jesus and of reflections of the significance of the incarnation have been bound into a collection of documents, known to us as the Bible. To varying degrees, Christians claim that these 'scriptures' are defining documents, enabling us to ground our moral and spiritual sense and to put real content to 'love'.

It seems to me that the outline above is both reasonable and necessary, *if God exists* and has, indeed, become incarnate as Jesus of Nazareth. An event as important as the incarnation would require historical 'preparation' in order for it to be understood. An account of the incarnation, as well as *definitive* reflections on its significance would be equally essential for the human race to become aware of what had occurred. Could all of this been done, however, without compromising human moral autonomy?

Christians view both the revelation found in the Bible and the means by which it has been recorded, in many different ways. On one extreme, some argue that God gave every Hebrew, Aramaic or Greek word directly to the authors of the Bible's various 'books' and that every word is quite literally 'the word of God', while at the other extreme, some view the Bible simply as a compilation of human reflections within a particular religious tradition. What might a *Christian* view of the Bible look like?

I should suggest that, from a *Christian* perspective, the writings contained in the Bible may be best understood as genuinely human, yet *God-infused*, responses to real acts of revelation of God to a particular people-group through a defined period of human history, culminating in the life, death and resurrection of Jesus of Nazareth. Again, whether or not it is reasonable to believe that God did, *in fact*, reveal God-self in the first instance, I shall discuss in the final section of this book.

It is clear to me that the Bible documents are very definitely documents of their times and that they ought not to be read as if they constitute some sort of uniform spiritual manual that can be consulted as if it was the direct creation of a single mind. The various authors and editors claim that events that they either witnessed, or that were part of their religious culture, revealed true aspects of God's nature, character and purposes. They detail, in the 'Old Testament', at various times in the history of the People of Israel, how communities responded as they attempted to be faithful to what they believed had been revealed to them. Sometimes the response may clearly be seen as reflecting aspects of God's character that we can recognise as being in keeping with the later teachings and example of Jesus; at other times the response falls well short of this mark. There is no doubt that as the Old Testament period progressed, so too did an understanding that God had revealed God-self not as a being that could appropriately be viewed merely as a powerful deity, but as a Supreme Being. With the record of the life, death and resurrection of Jesus and subsequent reflection on his significance, a much clearer image of God emerges; one that can be interpreted as being consistent with a Supreme Being.

If God exists and has revealed God-self in the history of Israel and supremely in the incarnation, then I believe that the Bible may reasonably be seen as combining both *witness and response* to that 'first-order' revelation. The 'Word of God' is a term used within the Bible to refer to God's self-revelation and so is used in an ultimate sense to refer to the incarnation. It is, therefore, I believe correct to say that the Bible is a *vehicle for communicating* the Word of God since it records and reflects on acts of God's self-revelation. This is not quite the same thing as saying that the Bible *is* the Word of God in the sense of it being a *direct act* of God's self-revelation. This is not to say, however, that it is not of unique value and significance. In that it identifies acts of God's self-revelation and then records ways in which faithful communities responded to it, it is invaluable. There is, however, more to be said.

The *process* of recording and reflecting on God's revelation (should such revelation have occurred) ought not, I believe, to be seen as something that God would simply leave to human endeavour without *appropriate* influence. It is clear that the final authors and editors of the various documents in the Bible believed that they were writing, in some sense, as ambassadors of God. This is also true of the communities, scholars and church leaders who, eventually compiled and identified the canon of the New Testament. It would be, I think, entirely incongruous, to argue that in doing so they failed to attempt to seek God's mind as they wrote or edited their material. *If God exists and if God has acted in self-revelation in the first place*, I should expect that the end product of this collaboration will be such that, at the very least, it bears trustworthy (though not necessarily 'literal') testimony to God's acts of revelation and that its reflections on the significance of God's revelation are uniquely significant in enabling me to understand God's nature, character and purposes. At the same time, the responses that are recorded are clearly human responses and are deeply influenced by their historical and cultural contexts. Of course, many Christians believe that the biblical documents are more than this, and they might be right. There is, however, no *requirement* for this to be the case.

This is a positive, not a negative, thing to note. It is entirely in keeping with humans being morally autonomous creatures that our understanding of God's revelation and our response to it will be couched in terms appropriate to their context. I cannot expect the People of Israel, whose lives were lived out in a perpetual war zone, resembling a cross between organised crime 'turf-wars' and 'total-war' in which genocide was a constant threat, to reflect the moral and social concerns of twenty first century suburbia. At the same time, their accounts of what they considered to be God's revelation and their responses to it are often light years ahead of anything that I would otherwise have expected from the era in which they are set. The fact that the final editors of the various Old Testament books chose to include details that were no longer of direct relevance to them in their particular historical contexts bears testimony to their desire to reflect faithfully the thoughts and actions of their forebears.

There is no doubt in my mind that many things accepted or condoned in some Old Testament passages, such as slavery, mass slaughter of enemies and enforced marriage of captive women are utterly and totally unacceptable and have no place in the mind or heart of God. Equally, hard as it is to accept, I have no doubt that given the bloody and brutal nature of life in the ancient world, it would have been extremely difficult for people living three thousand years ago to have realised this. Strange as it may seem, rejecting slavery, for example, would probably have been virtually unthinkable to them. This does not, of course, make slavery right (it is *entirely* wrong), but it does indicate that the Bible contains genuinely human responses to God's revelation; not thoughts 'parachuted' into the authors' minds by God. This is precisely what I should expect from a Supreme Being that has chosen to guide and not force us into recognising the truth.

An oft-quoted verse found in the New Testament document known as the second letter to Timothy contains the words, '*All Scripture is God-breathed (inspired) by God and profitable for teaching, for reproof, for correction, and for training in righteousness*'. This is, I believe a perfect *Christian* description of the Bible; it is profitable for all of the uses mentioned above and it emanates from God since it reflects God's self-revelation. There is also a continuing need to encounter God in and through its pages as its teachings are understood, interpreted and applied in changing contexts by understanding and appreciating the literary styles as well as the historical and cultural contexts in which the original documents were written.

Christian Living

I can imagine that what I have written with regard to the Bible, many Christians will dismiss as being hopelessly subjective and totally inadequate for enabling individuals and communities to discover and to understand very much at all about God's nature, character and purposes. Understandably, I beg to differ. It seems to me that a collection of writings, reflecting pivotal events, perceived to be acts of God's self-revelation, accompanied by honest accounts of how individuals and communities interpreted and responded to this revelation is of enormous value in enabling me to discern much about God.

If, *for the moment*, I assume that the Bible does, in fact, record real acts of revelation, centred on the ultimate revelation of God in the incarnation, this alone is of immeasurable benefit. The fact that such events are recorded for posterity enables me to engage with them, to be confronted by them and to be invited to respond to them. If the acts of revelation were not recorded, my spiritual quest would be hugely impoverished. Similarly, the accounts of how people throughout a period spanning well over one thousand years interpreted and interacted with God's self-revelation are of enduring value. More than that, I should like to think that when reading and reflecting on the Christian Scriptures, grappling with their messages and meanings, my search for truth is enabled and illuminated. Without accounts of God's revelation and how that revelation was received, reflected upon and responded to, both by the original and later generations of believers, I believe that I would often be left floundering.

None of this, however, means that I have to sign up to any of the, often conflicting, *theories* of inspiration or inerrancy that circulate within the Christian Church; I am happy simply to concur with the sentiments of the author of the second letter to Timothy, quoted above. So, for example, when one of the psalmists exclaims that whoever smashes the heads of his enemies' children against a rock is blessed by God (Psalm 137), I can appreciate this as a brutally honest cry of despair, but I am under no obligation to perform mental, moral and spiritual gymnastics to present it as reflecting the mind of God. Similarly, when the death penalty was invoked for a multitude of offences that threatened the 'purity' of Israelite religion, I can *understand* how this was deemed to be an appropriate response to the 'holiness' of God, by a nomadic group living under a constant threat of extinction by more powerful tribes whose moral, social and religious practices were such that burning children alive as sacrifices was seen as being not only acceptable, but mandatory. This does not mean, however, that I believe that the Bible ought to be used to support either capital punishment or religious intolerance.

I fully accept that when various laws were written in the name of God that the authors firmly believed that they were reflecting God's mind in their particular historical context. I suggest that if someone from the twenty-first century were to be catapulted back in time to live their lives immersed in that context, they too, might very well agree with the biblical authors. This does not mean, however, that what they wrote ought to be applied outside their original context and the ways in which ethical development can be traced throughout the Old Testament period suggests that other biblical authors concur. There is, for example, a clear tension between the legalistic lists of commands in books such as Leviticus and the later ethical imperatives of the prophetic books, requiring love and justice; mercy rather than sacrifice. The ways in which Jesus interpreted the Old Testament Law also suggest that he did not view its original interpretation and application as binding on his generation since he saw himself 'fulfilling' the Law. The captivating story of Jesus and the woman threatened with being stoned because she had committed adultery is a striking example of Jesus getting to the heart of what constitutes a proper response to God's holiness: a deep, personal and communal acknowledgement of the truly awful nature of human sinfulness. Understanding revelation is a progressive process. Finding an appropriate response to revelation entails adhering to *core principles* such as love and justice that can be identified as running throughout the Bible, but practices will vary according to context.

What this means for me as I seek to find out how to live a *Christian* life is that, *if it is true*, I shall take absolutely seriously, both the revelation contained in the Bible and the interpretation of that revelation and the responses that biblical individuals and communities made to it, in order to inform my own views and opinions. I shall not feel bound, however, to believe that every biblical verse expresses the mind of God or that all passages that were *entirely acceptable* in their original context ought to be applied today as if context was unimportant. The Bible does not claim such for itself; indeed, in a number of places biblical writers make a clear distinction between what they considered to be their own thoughts and commands from God. In short, I take the Bible much too seriously to take it literally.

My stance does require a lot of effort in trying to distinguish between what might reasonably be understood as revelation and what is better understood as interpretation and contextual application. Once again, however, I see this as a strength rather than as a weakness as it reflects the moral autonomy, essential for genuine faith. Truth to be told, even those who argue for belief in particular theories of inspiration and inerrancy disagree hugely with regard to how the Bible is to be interpreted and applied, so I am not at all sure that theories of biblical inspiration are of much practical use. *If God exists and has revealed God-self through events recorded in the Bible*, I can continue to read the Bible and find within it foundation testimony to God's self-revelation as well as immeasurably important interpretations of what this revelation means. Complemented by personal reflection, engagement with the views of others and current knowledge of history, science and other disciplines, the biblical witness provides a unique and definitive guide in my search for the truth.

Prayer

I have mentioned at a number of points in this book that my decisions and actions are not merely products of rational thinking, but that personal experience and intuition also play an essential role. Similarly, in trying to live a *Christian* life, to date, I have not simply engaged in mental reflection and intellectual discussion before deciding how to act. My background, my psychological profile, my physical abilities and limitations, my experiences of life and my intuition all contribute to making me who and what I am. So also has prayer: a practice based on the belief that I am able to communicate with God and that God is able to communicate with me. Perhaps because prayer is such a widely experienced and observed phenomenon, it is easy to forget that, *if well-founded*, it is really an astounding activity. Again, I shall explore in the final section of this book whether or not it is reasonable to believe that prayer can actually occur, and consequently whether or not prayer will continue to play a role in my life, but for the moment I wish to explore what prayer might entail, were it to be grounded in reality.

If prayer is understood merely as some sort of spiritual shopping expedition with humans asking God for such things as protection, success and happiness, then, while grave doubts might be expressed with regard to its efficacy, there is no difficulty in believing that prayer can occur. There is, after all, nothing stopping me from asking God to do me any number of favours. I may be seriously misguided in thinking that my requests will be successful and the high failure-rate of my prayers might cause me to question either the efficacy of prayer or the existence of God to whom I am praying, but the process of prayer, understood in this way, is a simple and uncomplicated one.

This, however, is not really what is meant by prayer, certainly not by those who have thought about it and practised it seriously. Many, perhaps most, of us have had the experience of panic-praying when faced with danger or significant problems; all we really want is for God to get us out of trouble. Such semi-automatic responses to crises are understandable, but they form only a small part of what the Christian tradition considers prayer to entail. Prayer is more fully understood as human beings communicating with God, with this communication taken to be a two-way process. Leaving to one side, for the moment, what such communication might actually effect, the issue that I wish to pursue, first of all, is how such communication might take place: how could we communicate with God and, perhaps more significantly, how could God communicate with us?

The first thing to say, I believe, is that prayer is, quite literally, all in the mind. This is not to suggest that it is not real, but that since the ultimate reality in a *Christian* worldview *is* mind, this is the appropriate 'place' for prayer to take place. If my mind exists within the mind of God and if God is always 'with' me, knowing and experiencing my every thought, this provides a platform for me to understand how prayer might work.

In terms of my communicating with God, prayer is essentially a matter of me realising that my every thought is known to God and that God experiences my thought processes with me. Whether I like it or not, my thoughts are completely accessible to God. My first goal in praying is, therefore, to be aware of this and to act accordingly. Making every thought a prayer is not a matter of rigorous self-discipline on my part, but rather, a matter of my recognising and making explicit what is already a fact. My thoughts are communicated to God all the time; it cannot be otherwise. My first role in praying is, therefore, to make this process a more conscious one. The fact that this does not feel as if there is some celestial eavesdropper snooping around my mind is, perhaps, an indication that living 'in the mind of God' is simply the natural way of living for human beings.

How though, might God communicate with me? The essential answer is, again, in and through my mind. Earlier, I suggested that

God's mind forms the essential mental and spiritual environment in which I live. Just as I am naturally affected by the physical environment around me, I will be similarly affected by this spiritual environment. My physical environment influences me; if it were not there or if it were different I should have either nothing or something different to which to respond. In a similar way, *if God exists*, God's existence gives me something to respond to mentally and spiritually. I may not always be aware of God's existence and so, I will not always be aware that I am responding to it. When I am aware of God's existence, however, I am able to respond to it in a more deliberate fashion. This, I suggest, is at the heart of prayer; not that God routinely pops words or thoughts into my mind, but that I become aware of God's presence and of God's essential nature. As I do so, perhaps with the right side of my brain helping me to 'sense' this spiritual environment and the left side of my brain helping me to 'make sense' of it, I am able, at least in part, to understand something of the mind of God. It is this two-way process of my thinking my thoughts before God and being aware of God's presence and nature as I reflect, that forms the basis of prayer. In this process, I believe that it is possible to speak of human beings experiencing the presence of God and communicating with God, without in any way suggesting that this experience proves God's existence. It is even possible for me to speak, in this way, of having a 'relationship' with God. All that I have described might, of course, simply be the workings of my own conscious and sub-conscious mind, but it *might not* be. It might reflect genuine communication with God.

If this is the essential nature of prayer, of what 'use' is it? How might it be best understood to help me in my quest to understand reality and to live the sort of life that God might want me to live?

I think that one understanding of prayer that I wish to jettison very quickly is the commonly held idea that prayer consists of humans making requests and God answering them, as if God were in charge of Customer Services in heaven. While asking God for things will, undoubtedly, form *part* of my relationship with God, it does not form the central part of it anymore than making requests forms the central part of my relationships with my wife or children. To treat God as some sort of answering machine is demeaning both to God and to me; a relationship with God is open to so many riches that to reduce it to a crass set of requests is, I believe, beyond credulity.

Moreover, it is, I think, abundantly clear that if prayer and my relationship with God essentially consist of my asking and God answering as I work my way through a wish-list, it has failed to produce the goods. In spite of game attempts by Christian writers and preachers to defend this sort of prayer by saying that God always answers with a 'yes', a 'no' or a 'not yet', I cannot see how it does not descend into God very arbitrarily choosing which of my and other people's requests to answer positively.

Prayer for healing is a good example. I have known literally hundreds of people who have asked God to heal them miraculously of their illnesses and I know of only a handful who can say that anything like a miraculous cure has resulted. Even then, their experiences fell short of being 'miracles', as popularly understood, since they could be explained with varying degrees of credibility in non-theistic terms. Similarly, people have prayed for God to protect them on their travels and have died in plane crashes, they have prayed for success in exams and have failed and they have prayed for financial blessings and have ended up being bankrupt. Of course, others have prayed in the same way and have had positive experiences, but unless God has favourites or *unless something else is involved*, it is unlikely that God has simply said 'yes' to some and 'no' to others. This is assuming that God is fair and that God does not play games with people's lives; a reasonable assumption, I believe, to make about a Supreme Being.

What I believe may happen when I pray is that *primarily*, God enables me to understand, to interpret and to experience things differently from the ways in which I would have experienced these things had I not prayed. This undoubtedly may result in my mind exerting a greater and more positive influence over my body and my circumstances than might have been the case if I had not prayed. The ways in which the human mind may interact with matter as well as with other minds is not at all understood. I believe that I ought to accept that the influence of a mind transformed through prayer might be, potentially, far-reaching. To dismiss some experiences of healing as being merely psychosomatic, for example, is to miss the point. All experiences of healing are *necessarily* psychosomatic since *all* human experiences are psychosomatic. It is entirely plausible that my mind, influenced through prayer, will have a positive, healing effect on my body and that, sometimes, this effect might even be thought of as being extraordinary. Such experiences will result from experiencing prayer as something that affects my mind and hence my body, not as slot-machine answers churned out in response to my requests and demands. The influence of my mind might even extend to influencing other minds and through them, other bodies.

The same is true, of course, for the mind of God, though to a much greater extent. The effects of my prayers might also involve God 'intervening' positively in the minds of others for whom I pray in a manner that does not negate their freewill. Prayer might enable me to make better decisions or to respond to 'hunches' that I would otherwise have ignored. In this way praying for safety as I travel is not a vain pursuit but my safety will still largely depend on me and others acting in a way that is in keeping with the mind of God (not speeding, not drinking alcohol and paying attention to what we are doing). This is not to say that God cannot and will not act in a *direct* manner if, presumably, it is either necessary or truly appropriate for God to do so (the incarnation is an example), but I suggest that these conditions are met relatively rarely. None of the above, however, ought to be understood as being automatic; prayer, *if it is real*, involves minds meeting and communicating and this is a personal rather than an automated process.

Some years ago I got into quite a bit of hot water by writing an article for an Irish Church magazine entitled, 'Should we stop praying for peace?' The point of the article was not that we ought to stop praying but that we ought to be praying differently: asking God to change our attitudes and behaviour rather that asking God to drop peace from the sky. I believe that it is reasonable to suggest that countless prayers for peace in Ireland have been answered in the sense that God's way was accepted by enough people to make peace possible, but I do not believe that God somehow withheld peace for three decades or more until God decided that we all had had enough of the violence and bloodshed.

I also believe that a good case may be made out for God answering the prayers of individuals in a way that is 'direct' for them but which will not necessarily appear to be direct to others. Such experiences must, however, not prove God's existence, even though they might give a great deal of confidence to the individuals concerned. It is clear, for example, that many people who have perished in war must have prayed for God to enable them to survive. It is equally clear that if God enabled everyone who prayed for survival to emerge intact from conflict, God's existence would be a demonstrable fact; the simplest of research projects would show that the survival rate of praying individuals was one hundred percent while the survival rate of non-prayers fell short of that mark. Similarly, if every road-crash victim that was prayed for made a complete recovery while some of those not prayed for died, God's existence would be beyond doubt. I have already outlined why such proof would undermine humans' ability to become genuinely moral beings, negating the entire reason behind the universe's existence. Such universal 'answers' to prayer are inimical both to the nature of God and to the moral development of human beings.

It *is* possible, however, for individuals to be influenced through prayer to act in certain ways that, on reflection, they realise enabled them to experience healing, protection or success. Had they not prayed, or had they not been prepared to respond to 'the mind of God' they would have acted differently, with different outcomes ensuing. If everyone was prepared to spend sufficient time praying before they acted, I am sure that the world would be a very different place, but of course, such is not the case. If it were, I suspect that no one would die as a result of conflict because there would be no conflict. I am not saying that this is all that can be said about the efficacy of prayer, but I suggest that understanding prayer as a two-way process of communication during which our minds may be influenced and through which our minds may then affect our bodies and the world around us is sufficient to indicate that prayer is both possible and potentially effective.

I have now reached a second watershed in my investigation. I believe that, so far, my enquiry suggests that *Christian* theology can be both coherent and possible. I now need to turn, in the third and final section of this book, to the all-important question of whether or not it is, in fact, believable.

Part Three

Might God be Real?

Chapter Thirteen

The Defining Issues
(Personal Prejudices… Reason, History, Intuition and Experience)

Clearing the Ground

Having reached this stage of my investigation, I am convinced that belief in the existence of God is plausible and that *Christian* theology is coherent; *neither, however, implies that it is true.* Before outlining factors that will help me decide whether or not *Christian* theology (or something like it) actually reflects reality, I need, first of all, to address some factors that I ought *not* to take into consideration. Unless these are properly identified and their potential influence acknowledged, they might manage to worm their way into my thinking as I try to reach my conclusions.

First among these is the persistent thought that physical materialism ought to be my default position and that the onus is on other theories, including theistic ones, to prove that they are right: in the absence of proof or at least of very strong evidence, I ought to stick to physical materialism. This bias, I know, is rationally unsustainable; it is simply a dogma and nothing more, but yet, I find that it has lodged itself in my mind with considerable tenacity. I have already argued that reality is of sufficient complexity and that I and other humans are of sufficiently limited intelligence to make a *dogmatic* assertion with regard to the nature of reality, unsustainable. The fact that at 'common sense' level I might observe reality in such a way that physical materialism appears to be a correct stating point for my investigation is irrelevant. Common sense has got very little to do with what physicists already know about the composition of the visible universe and it almost certainly has as little to do with the invisible universe of dark matter and dark energy. The only proper starting place for an investigation into the possible existence of God, and hence for Christian theology, is principled neutrality. I must not allow my psychological predisposition towards scepticism and my culturally influenced preference for atheism to get in the way, just as 'natural' theists ought not to begin with an assumption that God exists. This, I suspect will be easier said than done.

I also have to admit that I continue to be haunted by the spectre of gullibility. While atheism offers me an alluring degree of personal liberty and even of potential irresponsibility, should I choose to go down that road, I also recognise that, potentially, *Christian* theology offers me something even better in its vision of eternal life. It is my nature to be wary of anything that sounds too good to be true; I have been caught in my fair share of scams throughout my life and I have an inherent tendency to trust people, at times to find that my trust has been seriously misplaced. Consequently, I am genuinely wary of committing myself to any belief that offers 'eternal life'. This, however, is a matter of my personal psychology, based in part, on some negative experiences of broken trust. It is, frankly, irrelevant to the question of God's existence.

Finally, I have another nagging thought that clamours for my attention: the universe is both too big and too detailed for any being, even a Supreme Being, to be responsible for it and to 'inhabit' it. That God could know every experience of every creature, be aware of the movement of every electron and that God could also *care* about all of this is, almost beyond belief. I say 'almost' because I also recognise that if I were to make belief in such a Supreme Being unattainable I would be doing so purely on the basis of my own inability to appreciate all that a Supreme Being might be. The problem is not that a Supreme Being is too 'big'; it is that my mind is too small. I need to remind myself that I must not think of God as a bigger and better version of me or of God's mind as a 'super-brain'. If God exists and is Fundamental Mind, I cannot place any limits on God's mind; nor can I attempt to describe, never mind explain, how God thinks. There is no defensible reason for stating that a Supreme Being cannot be supreme.

So, with these mildly embarrassing admissions confessed and noted, I am ready to look at those areas that ought to be taken into consideration in determining whether or not *Christian* theology is believable.

Admissible Evidence

It is clear that my decision whether or not to belief in the existence of God and, consequently in *Christian* theology will be based, not on proof, but on evidence. As I have already suggested, this is the case for a number of reasons. In the first instance, if proof, one way or the other, existed it is most likely that it would have been discovered by now; the fact that books like this one can be written suggests that such has not been the case. Equally importantly, *if* God exists as a Supreme Being and *if* God has created semi-autonomous moral beings, then, as I have argued earlier, proof of God's existence is inimical to these propositions. Similarly, *if* God does not exist, how could I possibly prove the non-existence of a being whose existence, by definition, lies beyond scientific verification?

In weighing evidence for and against the existence of God and of the veracity of *Christian* theology, philosophical and scientific reasoning can only take me so far. They can demonstrate that the existence of God is plausible and that *Christian* theology is coherent, but they cannot really go beyond this. I acknowledge this fact with a degree of irritation; it would be so much easier if I were able to use reason and the scientific method alone to settle the issue. I am convinced, for reasons that I have outlined in the previous two sections of this book, that this is not possible. Where else then, might I look for evidence?

There are, I believe, three main avenues open to me: 'foundational' Christian history, intuition and experience. It would, of course, be impossible for me to survey all of human history or to attempt a critique of all human experiences. For reasons that I have mentioned already, I intend to look first of all at the foundational history of the Christian tradition. I shall then view whatever provisional conclusions this may lead me to make, through the prisms of intuition and experience.

I hope through this process to discover whether or not I am still by temperament and inclination an atheist, but by persuasion, a *Christian*.

Chapter Fourteen

Foundational Christian History –
The Resurrection of Jesus

(The New Testament Documents… The New Testament Environment…
Paul and the Resurrection… Possible Interpretations of the Resurrection…
The 'Appearance' Narratives… The Empty Tomb Narratives…
Resurrection Faith)

I cannot escape the fact that Christian history is focused on the reputed actions and sayings of Jesus of Nazareth and that the single most important event in his personal history is his alleged resurrection from the dead. All that comes before this personal history in the Old Testament may be seen as being preparatory to it and all that follows may be seen as being dependent upon it. Clearly, I cannot escape looking, in some depth, at the topic of Jesus' resurrection if I am serious in evaluating the veracity of *Christian* theology.

The importance of the resurrection of Jesus goes beyond a study of theology. If it occurred in *anything like* the manner understood by traditional Christianity, then it is the single most important event in the history of the human race and it has the most profound implications for my understanding of reality. If Jesus rose from the dead then it is reasonable for me to believe that a personal, conscious life beyond death is possible. It will also encourage me to find out as much as I can about the life, character and teachings of Jesus, treating them with the utmost seriousness and respect. While it may be theoretically possible to adopt an atheist understanding of the resurrection by viewing Jesus' experience as an extremely rare event caused by unknown natural laws and forces, it seems to me that this would be a rather desperate attempt to avoid theism. In short, if I come to believe that the resurrection of Jesus occurred, I am forced to reassess just about everything in my life, including my attitude to the existence of God. Equally, if I come to believe that the resurrection did not occur in the sense that Jesus continued to live as a transformed human person after his crucifixion, that too, will have the most profound implications for my belief in the existence or non-existence of God.

At this point I must stress that I am definitely not going to slip into some sort of Christian apologetic, trying to prove that the resurrection happened. In this enquiry I am interested in *investigating* the alleged event; not in *defending* it. Nonetheless, I embark on this investigation with a proper appreciation of the importance of the subject.

The New Testament

In assessing the resurrection of Jesus, the first thing that strikes me, is that all relevant information comes from the pages of the New Testament. While it would have been ideal if some contemporary non-Christian references to the resurrection existed, I do not consider their absence to constitute a major problem since, in fairness, it is difficult to see where else, other than within Christian circles, such information might be found. No one at the time of Jesus' crucifixion believed that he was going to occupy more than the smallest of foot-notes in the history of the Jewish People or that he would have appeared at all in a history of the Roman Empire. Even when his disciples began to preach that he had risen from the dead, initially all that happened was that a small sect developed within Judaism. There were many such sects and movements whose names have long been lost to posterity. Similarly, the Roman Empire was home to, literally, hundreds, if not thousands, of religious groups, each with its devotees and missionaries. Christianity did not make a discernible impact within the Roman Empire until twenty years or more after Jesus' crucifixion and probably was not seen as a potentially threatening and unsettling influence until the time of Nero, some thirty years after the events recorded in the Gospels. Only then, is it reasonable to believe that increasing references to Christianity might be found among non-Christian writers; which is, in fact, what happened.

The only information with regard to the alleged resurrection that I can take seriously is information that comes from the first generation of Christian disciples who claimed either to have encountered the risen Jesus personally or to have been personally influenced by those claiming to have had such encounters. The comments and views, both of later supporters and later detractors of Christianity alike, might be interesting, but they do not contribute anything significant to my quest. Such comments were built on their knowledge of the lives and writings of first generation Christians; unless they can provide me with some accurate, fresh information not contained in the New Testament, my focus must return to those documents. To date, since no such information has been found, I remain unmoved by the excitement sometimes evident when scholars or popular religious writers purport to have unearthed important information about the origins of Christianity because they have discovered or rediscovered writings from the second or third centuries.

I am, therefore, left with the New Testament documents. They are, of course, biased in that they were written and edited by individuals and communities that were Christian, even though I also recognise that some individuals, such as the important leaders Paul and James, were *not* followers of Jesus prior to his alleged resurrection. Moreover, the New Testament authors make no secret of the fact that their writings were designed either to engender belief in Jesus as 'Lord' or to encourage existing believers in their faith. The Gospels, for example, may appropriately be termed 'propaganda': documents with carefully chosen content; crafted and designed to elicit a positive response from their readers. In the epistles, the authors were, quite literally preaching to the converted. In investigating whether or not the resurrection occurred, I must begin by recognising that such are the only primary source documents that I have at my disposal. I might wish that it were otherwise, but wishful thinking will not get me any further in my enquiry.

There is, of course, no question of my starting from the proposition that the New Testament documents are inspired by God and are, therefore, trustworthy. This sort of circular reasoning abounds in many Christian circles. The possibility that the New Testament documents are in any way 'inspired' depends on God existing and, I have suggested, a defensible starting place for looking at evidence for God's *actual* existence is the resurrection of Jesus. As the New Testament documents constitute the core evidence for belief in the resurrection I must treat them as I would any historical documents from that time; with proper academic rigour. There can be no question of any special pleading for them.

Detailed study of the origins of the New Testament documents is almost as complex as a study of physics and almost as inaccessible to all but those specifically trained in its methods. Nonetheless, like physics, the research of scholars has been distilled into forms that are palatable to interested students and observers. The approach that I am going to take in utilising the New Testament documents to assess the resurrection may be described as being one of *reasoned criticism*. That is to say, because the issue is so important, I am choosing to follow the findings of those scholars who, in their writings, appear to make genuine efforts neither to defend nor to attack the New Testament documents simply because of their personal philosophical or theological convictions. Happily for me, such scholars do exist. I am aware that this will have the effect of placing my enquiry more towards the 'critical' than the 'conservative' end of New Testament studies and that, by so doing I might ignore some good conservative arguments. This is a price that I am happy to pay; *if* I come to the conclusion that the resurrection of Jesus happened, I want to ensure that it may not be undermined because, unwittingly, I accepted something on faith rather than on its evidential value. *If* there is a place for faith, it ought to be at *the end* of a process of enquiry, not during the enquiry itself. In my investigation of the resurrection, I am not arguing that measured critical scholarship is necessarily always right, but rather that it forms a defensible starting point for my enquiry.

As I have stated, the study of how and why the New Testament documents have taken their present form is a demanding one and it is not possible in this chapter to do more than outline my understanding of current developments in this field. While the canon of the New Testament was not widely accepted as comprising the twenty seven 'books' found in modern Bibles until the end of the fourth century, scholarly opinion accepts that the core documents of the synoptic Gospels (Matthew, Mark and Luke) and some of Pauls' letters (Romans, First and Second Corinthians, First Thessalonians, Galatians, Philippians and Philemon) were written and circulated within fifty to sixty years of the crucifixion. The Acts of the Apostles comes from the same pen as Luke's Gospel and provides important information with regard to the emergence of the primitive Christian Church. It seems reasonable to me, therefore, to base my enquiry on these core documents. This is not to say that the Church was mistaken to accept other 'books' into the canon of the New Testament or that it is certain that they are not authentic early Christian documents. Belief in something as fundamental as the resurrection, however, can only be based on documentary evidence that is *undisputedly* early (within half a century or so, of the crucifixion) and that can be *undisputedly* identified with the *earliest* followers of Jesus. It is also fair to point out that those New Testament documents lying outside the core documents that I have listed all bear the same emphasis on the importance of the resurrection as do these core documents. Other early Christian documents, both those considered orthodox (such as the Epistle of Barnabas) and those believed to be heterodox (such as the Gospel of Thomas) do not meet the criteria of being undisputedly early and of being undisputedly identified with the earliest followers of Jesus.

Some of the core documents are very early indeed, with Paul's letters being written between twenty and thirty years after the crucifixion and, in a number of places, incorporating earlier written material from other sources. The synoptic Gospels were probably edited in their final form between thirty and fifty years after the crucifixion; the Acts of the Apostles shortly after. (The Gospel of John, which I am not treating as a primary source document in this enquiry because of lack of scholarly consensus, might have been composed anywhere between twenty and seventy years after Jesus' death.) The range of possible dates for the publication of the Gospels results from scholars' various analyses of the processes involved in their composition. In addition to these undisputed core documents, other earlier documents existed but have either been lost (for example the Gospel source document, 'Q') or parts of them have been incorporated into canonical documents (such as parts of Paul's letters to the churches in Corinth and Philippi). It is certainly widely accepted that the Gospel writers used earlier written and as well as oral sources and Paul refers to other letters that he wrote which are now lost to us, as well as reflecting in at least one of his letters, early Aramaic liturgical material that emanated from the primitive Judean church.

In comparison to other documents from the ancient world that purport to record historical events, the synoptic Gospels and Paul's letters are very close to the lifetime of Jesus. Josephus, the Jewish historian, for example, mentions John the Baptist as well as Jesus (in a passage that was probably altered by later Christian scribes), but he wrote over sixty years after the events he was describing. Suetonius wrote of Julius Caesar more than one hundred and sixty years after the dictator's death, while Tacitus wrote of the emperor Augustus, after a lapse of more than one hundred years. Temporal distance from the events that historians record is not, necessarily, a problem; if I think of modern events such as the Second World War, many excellent histories have been published fifty years and more after the end of the war. Time is needed for compilation of sources, for reflection and analysis before notable publications emerge. A bald chronology of events supplies me with little more than a time-line and is almost useless in helping me to understand the past.

I do not find it surprising therefore, that Paul did not write letters to various churches until he was established in his role as a missionary to the Gentiles or that only some of his letters were kept for posterity. The undisputed letters that we do have provide a fascinating insight into the world of the first generation of Christian believers. Historians would dearly love to find letters of similar interest, written or dictated by Paul's contemporaries such as Boudica or Nero and would most certainly treat them as absolute treasures. Similarly, as long as the Gospels are understood to be documents that seek to encourage people to follow Jesus, there is nothing unusual in such definitive documents emerging up to fifty or sixty years after Jesus death. The use that the writers and editors of the Gospels made of earlier written and oral source material is, itself, a fascinating study, but the finished documents are unique in providing carefully fashioned *interpretations* of the life of Jesus that were widely accepted by the early Christian communities.

The New Testament Environment

Before looking at Paul's writings and the Gospels (supplemented by extracts from the Acts of the Apostles), I believe that a little more 'clearing of the ground' needs to be done. In attempting to assess the first Christians' understanding of the resurrection I think that it is important to place them in their proper historical, religious and cultural context. It would be a gross error to assume that the first disciples were ignorant, superstitious and unsophisticated. The fishermen followers of Jesus were businessmen, Matthew was a civil servant, John was associated with the aristocratic echelons of the temple administration in Jerusalem and Paul was an urbane Roman Citizen with a skilled legal and philosophical mind. They almost certainly all spoke Greek as well as Aramaic and some, at least, were able to read Hebrew. They lived at a time when communication and transport throughout the Roman Empire were well-developed and ideas were widely circulated. Art, literature, architecture and the theatre flourished. It would be entirely wrong to dismiss the first disciples as being strangers to reason; the study of the physical sciences, mathematics and philosophy were advanced, limited only by lack of technological prowess. In many ways, the world of the Roman Empire, heavily influenced by Hellenism, represented a society that was not to be matched for its sophistication and diversity in Europe until well into the eighteenth century. Sadly, the relative stagnation that engulfed Europe for centuries following the collapse of the Roman Empire was due, in part, to the stifling effects of the Christian Church, but I cannot blame the first generation of Christians for their successors' failings. Of course, the Roman Empire was also home to brutality, corruption and superstition, but then again, so too is the world of the twenty-first century.

The Palestinian background of the very first disciples suggests that they must have been naturally hostile to anything that could have compromised their monotheistic faith, the importance of the temple or belief that the Hebrew Scriptures (particularly the Torah) were definitive and complete religious texts. At the very least, the resurrection carried with it implications that must have stretched them in all these areas. At the same time, Hellenistic Jews had access to theologically speculative thought that would have enabled them to explore the implications of the resurrection with some degree of dexterity.

The world of the first Christians was, therefore, a complex and diverse one; there are no grounds for dismissing them as ignorant or primitive people. This, I believe, will have an important bearing on my appreciation of what they meant when they proclaimed the resurrection of Jesus

Paul and the Resurrection

Along with the significance of the crucifixion, the resurrection lies at the heart of Paul's understanding of the gospel and this is reflected throughout his writings. It is simply not possible to make any sense at all of his epistles without acknowledging that he was absolutely and totally convinced of the resurrection of Jesus. Precisely what he understood resurrection to entail is open to discussion, but his belief in its reality is beyond doubt. For Paul it was the case that without the resurrection there could be no authentic Christian faith.

In examining Paul's belief in the resurrection, it is fortunate for enquirers that he devoted a significant section of one of his letters (1 Corinthians 15) to the topic, underlining its significance for him. It is, I believe, impossible to read this passage without being impressed by the *absolute* nature of his belief in the resurrection's reality. He is quite explicit: if the resurrection did not happen, Christians have believed in vain in Jesus, they are still 'in their sins' and they are to be pitied more than any other group of people on earth; they are fools that have been duped. These are not the sentiments of a man who harboured any doubts.

In his Corinthian correspondence, Paul was writing to Christians who had already accepted the gospel message that he had preached. He does not, therefore, present the gospel to them again in detail, although he often alludes to it or discusses some of its theological implications. Similarly, apart from a direct reference to Jesus' words during the Last Supper and frequent references to the crucifixion, Paul does not quote any of Jesus' teaching, nor does he give us any biographical information about Jesus. This does not necessarily mean, however, that he was unfamiliar with such details.

While Paul, the pastor and teacher, does not engage in gospel preaching in his epistles, the Acts of the Apostles may be seen as giving its readers some authentic insight into the preaching of Paul the missionary. If Acts does contain essentially reliable information about Paul, he was, indeed, aware of Jesus' mission and ministry. Paul's focus, nonetheless, was firmly on the *risen Christ* (although he does use the name, 'Jesus' frequently) and on the 'saving' significance of Jesus' death in the light of the resurrection.

What this means for my investigation into Paul's understanding of the resurrection is that I have to be careful in building any 'arguments from silence'. I must assume *neither* knowledge nor ignorance on Paul's behalf with regard to information found in the Gospels. Difficult as it is, I must assess Paul's writings in their own right. While an argument can reasonably be advanced (without insisting that Luke produces verbatim reports of Paul's speeches) that our knowledge of his faith can be fleshed out from the accounts of his teaching found in the Acts of the Apostles, it is important, first of all, to assess Paul's epistles as they stand.

In writing to the Christians in Corinth, Paul expands a formula that was almost certainly in existence from the earliest days of the Christian Church and states that *'Christ died for our sins in accordance with the Scriptures, that he was buried, that he was raised on the third day in accordance with the Scriptures, and that he appeared to Cephas, then to the twelve. Then he appeared to more than five hundred brothers at one time, most of whom are still alive, though some have fallen asleep. Then he appeared to James, then to all the apostles. Last of all, as to one untimely born, he appeared also to me.'* (1 Corinthians 15: 3-8).

In his epistle to the church in Galatia, Pauls begins a defence of his apostleship and understanding of the gospel by writing, *'For I would have you know, brothers, that the gospel that was preached by me is not man's gospel. For I did not receive it from any man, nor was I taught it, but I received it through a revelation of Jesus Christ. You have heard of my former life in Judaism, how I persecuted the church of God violently and tried to destroy it. And I was advancing in Judaism beyond many of my own age among my people, so extremely zealous was I for the traditions of my fathers. But when he who had set me apart before I was born, and who called me by his grace, was pleased to reveal his Son to me, in order that I might preach him among the Gentiles, I did not immediately consult with anyone; nor did I go up to Jerusalem to those who were apostles before me, but I went away into Arabia, and returned again to Damascus.'* (Galatians 1: 11-17)

As many commentators have noted, Paul does not mention the empty tomb in these passages, although he does mention the burial of Jesus as well as indicating that the resurrection took place 'on the third day' (presumably after the crucifixion). As indicated above, this might mean that he was not aware of accounts of an empty tomb or it could be that he assumed that his readers already knew of such reports and understood that it could be inferred from references to burial and to resurrection 'on the third day'. Paul does not supply any detail with regard to the nature, content or duration of the 'appearances' of Jesus, although he does indicate that, in its timing, the revelation of Jesus to him stands apart from the experiences of others.

As stated above, in his letter to the Corinthians, Paul initially repeats a formula that had been given to him, presumably by the first apostles whom, in his letter to the Galatians he explained, he visited on a number of occasions subsequent to his conversion. At the same time, he is adamant in the Galatian epistle that his experience of the risen Jesus did not require any validation from others. What is certain is that Paul believed that his experience and the experience of other apostles and disciples were such that he and they were totally convinced of the resurrection of Jesus.

In the Corinthian letter (chapter 15), Paul expands a little on his understanding of the nature of the resurrection. Without reproducing the entire chapter here, I think that it is fair to say that Paul rules out an understanding of the resurrection that interprets it simply as the continuing influence of Jesus' teaching and life; rather, the resurrection is an event that led Jesus into *a continued and transformed state of existence*. At the same time, he insists that the 'resurrection body' is not 'natural', but 'spiritual'. He speaks of resurrection in terms of a 'spiritual body', contrasting it with a body of 'flesh and blood'.

The contrast between 'natural' and 'spiritual' is not a simple contrast between 'physical' and 'non-physical', but reflects a distinction between what might be seen as being intrinsically part of common human experience and what might be seen as belonging specifically to the actions of God on human experience. Nonetheless, it is not possible to dismiss entirely the 'material/immaterial' contrast. I think, therefore, that it is reasonable to interpret Paul's words as indicating, *at the very least*, that he understood Jesus' *person* to continue to exist with the same essential mind as prior to his death, but with an objective, personal and identifiable 'expression' that better reflected the nature of his mind. This, I believe, is the 'minimum' understanding of resurrection that may be seen as reflecting Paul's thought. It might be possible to go further and argue that the risen Jesus is still a *psychosomatic* unity, but that requires further exploration.

This interpretation of Paul's teaching seems to me to represent a defensible, if minimal, understanding of resurrection. *If* the essential nature of the universe is mind and *if* God exists, there is no reason why such a transformed existence should not be possible. Of course, my belief in the existence of God is deeply influenced by whether or not the resurrection actually occurred. I cannot simply say that because I can appreciate what sort of experience resurrection might be that it, therefore, happened and that God, therefore, exists. I need to examine further, why Paul was so certain that the resurrection of Jesus had, in fact, occurred.

It is clear from his writings, that Paul's 'conversion' experience on the road from Jerusalem to Damascus was pivotal in him coming to believe in the resurrection with such absolute certainty that it led him to abandon his career within orthodox Judaism and even to embrace belief in Jesus' divinity. These were huge steps for Paul to have taken and they bear testimony to the depth of his belief in the resurrection, as do his many experiences of hardship and persecution as a Christian missionary. They do not, however, furnish me with any further details with regard to the resurrection event itself or to the nature of Paul's encounter with the risen Jesus.

It is worth noting, nonetheless, that Paul clearly distinguished his encounter with Jesus on the road to Damascus from subsequent visions, dreams and altered-consciousness states that he experienced, some of which he wrote about in his letters (2 Corinthians 12) and some of which are recounted by the author of the Acts of the

Apostles (Acts 27). While this is significant in that it makes it difficult to dismiss Paul's encounter with Jesus as belonging to any of these categories, it still does not tell me anything about the nature of the encounter itself. For further insight, I have to turn to the accounts of Paul's conversion, found in the Acts of the Apostles where the story is recounted no fewer than three times (chapters 9, 22 and 26); an indication of its importance for Paul's faith and an indication of the importance of Paul's faith for the expansion of the Christian Church into the Gentile world.

In turning to the Acts of the Apostles, I accept (though I cannot prove) either that Luke recorded the essential features of Paul's conversion accurately or that he supplied accounts that he believed accurately reflected Paul's understanding of his encounter with the 'Risen Jesus'. As these accounts are not, by any means, simple reflections of the resurrection appearance stories found in the Gospels (including those recorded by Luke), it seems reasonable to suggest that Luke has written with deliberation and care and that his accounts ought to be treated accordingly.

The first thing that strikes me when I read the relevant passages in the Acts of the Apostles is that there are variations of detail in the three recorded accounts of Paul's experience. Bearing in mind that scholarly consensus indicates that a single author/editor (Luke) was responsible for the production of Acts and that he was probably a companion of Paul on some of his missionary journeys, I acknowledge that these differences did not cause him to doubt the credibility of Paul's conversation story. He was clear about the central event itself: Paul believed that he had an encounter with the risen Jesus on his way to Damascus from Jerusalem and this encounter was the defining moment of his life.

In reading the accounts of Paul's encounter with Jesus, recorded in the Acts of the Apostles, it appears to me that it is presented as an event during which he was enabled to experience *something* that he would otherwise have been *naturally* unable to have experienced. It was as if he was able to see ultra-violet light or dark matter; the experience is not presented as imaginary, but *it was not wholly accessible to others*. The accounts in the Acts of the Apostles make it clear that, at most, Paul's companions on the road to Damascus saw a bright light and heard 'the sound of a voice', but did not understand what the voice said. Paul, however, heard intelligible words being addressed specifically to him. The experience was undoubtedly understood *by Paul* as an encounter with a transformed Jesus, thus confirming his resurrection. It is, I think, testimony to Luke's desire to communicate what he understood to have actually happened, that he did not claim that, at any time, Paul *saw* Jesus.

As I have already observed, this was to be the pivotal moment in Paul's life; from this point on his beliefs and his actions were based firmly on the conviction that Jesus had been resurrected. For example, the remarkable hymn of praise, ascribing divinity to Jesus, included in the second chapter of Paul's letter to the church at Philippi (most probably a Greek translation of a very early Aramaic hymn) cannot be understood other than in the light of belief in the resurrection. It seems to me that such deeply ingrained belief in the resurrection, shared by Paul and the other early disciples, cannot have occurred unless *something* extraordinary had happened. The question is: what was it? What was the nature of the event that convinced Paul and others that Jesus was alive? What, in fact, *did* they mean when they spoke of resurrection?

Possible Interpretations of Resurrection

Paul's writings and the accounts of his conversion experience recorded in the Acts of the Apostles can, reasonably, be interpreted to support three varying interpretations of the resurrection. Which one Paul might have subscribed to is, of course, a matter of debate. In the first instance, they can be understood to support a 'traditional' view of the resurrection: Jesus died and was buried and on the third day after his burial, his tomb was found to be empty because he had risen *physically* from the dead. On that day, and for a few weeks following, his disciples had a series of encounters with him. While being recognisably identifiable with Jesus of Nazareth he was now alive as a 'transformed' human being. The resurrection was a factual occurrence that included a transformation in the physical corpse of Jesus; hence I shall term this a *'transformed physical'* understanding of the resurrection.

Alternatively, based *purely* on Pauls' writings and the accounts of his conversion in the Acts of the Apostles, it is also possible to conclude that the resurrection was an essentially *non-physical* event. That is to say, as a consequence of a series of experiences following his crucifixion, understood to be encounters with Jesus, Paul and other disciples were convinced that Jesus truly survived physical death and continued to live in a state that transcended his previous mode of existence. Jesus survived death in a personally identifiable form, able to communicate with his disciples; he was not simply a 'realised memory' or a ghostly imprint. The resurrection took place, though it did not, *in itself*, affect his corpse. It enabled him to continue to live in a state that lay closer to the immaterial than the material end of the spectrum of reality.

This could mean that Jesus continued to exist as a 'mind' within the mind of God, and that the disciples, through a series of visions, were given 'access' to this reality. This understanding of the resurrection, I am going to term, *'spiritual resurrection'*.

A non-physical interpretation of the resurrection, however, does not *necessarily* imply this form of 'spiritual resurrection'. It can also be presented as indicating a 'hyper-physical' existence, akin to that espoused by the traditional understanding of the resurrection, the essential difference being that the physical corpse of Jesus was not transformed. In other words, Jesus continued to live in a manner that was markedly different from his pre-resurrection experience, but which was still capable of being 'localised' in time and space. This understanding of the resurrection, I am going to term, *'hyper-physical resurrection'*.

I believe that all of these interpretations of the resurrection are consistent with (or to put it negatively, do not contradict) what we know of *Paul's* reported experience of the resurrection although, of course, that does not mean to say that *any of them* reflects the reality of what (if anything) happened on the first Easter.

While I do not believe that it accurately reflects Paul's thinking, others of course, have gone further than a 'spiritual' understanding of the resurrection and view all resurrection references as purely symbolic ways of stating that Jesus' influence continued after his death; the original, symbolic nature of the resurrection language later becoming, mistakenly, to be interpreted literally by many Christians. In all honesty, I find it impossible to read Paul's epistles in this way; the resurrection is simply too important in Paul's thought for me to take seriously that this is what he understood resurrection to mean.

A number of fringe theories also abound that attempt to 'demystify' the resurrection: the disciples deliberately lied about the resurrection or they haplessly misunderstood a series of encounters with a number of mysterious individuals as meetings with Jesus. Equally far-fetched, are theories suggesting that Jesus never died or that his body was stolen by the Jewish authorities who, for some reason, preferred the disciples propagating the message of the resurrection to their attempting to set the record straight. While, of course, no theory, however improbable can be disproved, I find all of these fringe theories utterly inadequate to explain the existence and development of the Christian Church and its rapid expansion; an expansion so rapid that within twenty years of Jesus' death it was possible for the emperor Claudius to identify Christians as a group significant enough to warrant expulsion from Rome. They also fail to reflect the seriousness and conviction with which the resurrection is uniformly portrayed in the New Testament documents and its absolute centrality for Christian faith; a faith that the early followers of Jesus were prepared to suffer and die for without any prospect of financial, political or social gain. When I take the time to read Paul's letters as well as accounts of early Christian preaching contained in the Acts of the Apostles, I confess that these theories appear to be very threadbare indeed.

The essence of Paul's preaching of the resurrection was that God had validated Jesus' life and message by demonstrating that he continued to live, beyond death, in a conscious and transformed human state. The demonstration of this resurrected life came in a series of encounters which his disciples found so overwhelming that they were entirely convinced that Jesus was, indeed, alive in a transformed state. Consequently, they not only believed in what he had taught, but they came to see him as being God-incarnate, the Saviour of the human race and the focal point of human history. It seems to me, to be beyond doubt that the reported encounters between Jesus and his disciples were, *in Paul's opinion*, both real and of ultimate significance. I can find nothing in the rest of the New Testament to suggest that any early Christians took an alternative view.

I think that I can, therefore, entirely dismiss the ideas that the New Testament understanding of the resurrection can be portrayed as meaning that Jesus' life, teaching and example continued to influence his followers in a uniquely powerful way after his death or that they were so desperate to continue the 'Jesus project' that they simply invented the whole resurrection story. It is difficult to see why (in contrast to the followers of many other 'failed messiahs') they did not simply accept that they had been wrong, unless some highly unusual event or series of events convinced them that Jesus' death did not, in fact, represent a tragic end, not only to Jesus' life, but also to many of his disciples' hopes. As I have said, I think that *something* had to happen to cause Christianity to explode upon history with such vibrancy and tenacity; *something* had to happen to give the first disciples their unshakeable belief that Jesus was alive.

The Nature of the Resurrection and the Appearance Narratives

As I have already acknowledged, that something *could* have been a physical resurrection. This has been the traditional understanding of the resurrection throughout the Church's history and it reflects a 'straightforward' reading of the Gospels; certainly had that occurred, the disciples faith is readily understandable. Such might, indeed, have been the case and, in the absence, of any serious alternative explanations for the first disciples' faith, I should feel obliged either to believe it or to reject the disciples' accounts as simple fabrication, something that I have already dismissed as being highly unlikely. Other interpretations of the resurrection *are*, however, available, including the alternatives of 'non-physical resurrection' and hallucination which, I believe, deserve careful examination.

Non-Physical Resurrection

Looking first at *accounts of encounters* with the 'Risen Jesus', I noted above, that in the Acts of the Apostles, Paul's encounter with Jesus was presented as something that only he fully experienced; he alone was able to hear Jesus' voice even though he did not see him. Turning to the Gospels, it is interesting to note that in Luke's Gospel (chapter 24), the account of two disciples meeting Jesus on the road from Jerusalem to Emmaus, is characterised by them not recognising him until their 'eyes were opened'. Matthew's Gospel (chapter 28) also records that when a group of disciples met with Jesus in Galilee, many believed, but some still doubted. While not including John's Gospel as an undisputedly early document, I also recognise that John (chapter 20) presents Mary Magdalene as mistaking Jesus for a gardener until she hears him call her by name. The disciples first of all dismissed her account and then later believed that they had seen a ghost when Jesus appeared to them, before finally believing in the resurrection. In his post-script (chapter 21), John records a story of some of Jesus' disciples meeting him at the lake-shore in Galilee in which he states that they did not dare to ask Jesus who he was, but that they knew it was 'the Lord'.

That these honest admissions of misunderstanding, doubt and mystery are recorded in the Gospels speaks highly of the integrity of their authors and editors. If they had simply been fabricating their accounts, passing them off as 'objective proofs' of the resurrection, it would have been so much easier for them to have removed all ambiguity. This does not mean that the accounts are necessarily to be understood as 'factual reports' in the sense understood in the twenty first century, but neither does it mean that the Gospel writers can easily be dismissed as deliberately creating and then *falsifying* legend as fact.

In the light of this, *one* plausible interpretation of the resurrection narratives is that the encounters of the first disciples with Jesus reflect *real, though non-physical* events. While they were *essentially* mental (spiritual) events, they may be distinguished from *purely subjective* mental events in that the disciples encountered something (someone) that *truly* existed. These experiences, however, were not always shared by all others present and the significance of them was not always immediately apparent (Paul's experience surpassed that of his companions, Matthew speaks of believers *and* doubters, the 'revelation' to Luke's travellers took place at the end of their encounter). These narratives may, reasonably, be accounted for in two possible ways.

In the first instance the Gospel narratives might reflect *actual* memories of the first disciples, in which case, were we to be able to go back in time and film the encounters, we might possibly see the disciples acting in a very peculiar manner, focusing on and relating to someone that *they* could clearly 'see', but which could not be captured by our hypothetical camera. Secondly, the narratives might be *stylised* accounts, *indicative* of the disciples' experiences, rather than *reports* of these experiences. In this case, the reality consisted of a series of individual and communal experiences, (perhaps, loosely termed 'visionary' in nature, though not subjective in origin) during which the identity and significance of the risen Jesus became apparent to the disciples, but which are presented in the Gospels as stylised, abbreviated and, perhaps, conflated narratives. In either case, the accounts originated *outside* the minds of the disciples and testify to real encounters with a resurrected Jesus.

Hallucination

I also accept that, as with a 'transformed physical' interpretation of the resurrection these experiences *could* have been the purely *psychological* products of individual and communal hallucinations, originating *within* the minds of the disciples. One problem with any such 'psychological theory', however, is that, as far as I am aware, the disciples' *recorded* experiences do not readily conform to the known pathology of 'normal' hallucinations. Many commentators have pointed out that the experiences were both individual *and communal* in their occurrence. With the exception of Paul's singular experience, they all occurred within a brief time-frame, ending quite abruptly a few weeks after the crucifixion. They were protracted and coherent encounters and they were experienced by people with a wide variety of psychological profiles, including some individuals who were either indifferent or hostile to Jesus and they were so convincing that they formed the basis of a new religion whose first adherents were prepared to sacrifice everything, including their lives, in order to proclaim the message of the resurrection. Furthermore, they were centred on something that the first disciples *and their first converts* would have found inherently difficult to believe: a crucified man had risen from the dead and had entered into a transformed state of existence.

Of course, it is also possible that the recorded experiences were *stylised* accounts of an original series of hallucinations. This would remove some of the above obstacles, though not all. It still leaves open, for example, questions of the cause and nature of hallucinations that were powerful enough to convince a disparate group of hitherto disconsolate, indifferent or hostile individuals.

The authors of the Gospels would have known nothing of the insights of modern psychology in general, or of the findings of experiments into hallucinations in particular, and so could not have written their narratives in such a way as to take 'hallucination theory' into account. Whatever underlies the appearance narratives, I do not think that they represent a deliberate attempt by the Gospel authors to make use of their knowledge of psychology. In order to argue that the appearance narratives (including Paul's encounter) were based on purely subjective, naturally induced hallucinations, I should have to postulate that the disciples' original experiences did, in fact, conform to what we know of hallucinations, but that, *by chance*, these experiences were recorded in such a way that they appear *not to* conform to what we know of the occurrence of hallucinations.

For example, perhaps there were one or more communal hallucinations, shared by disciples with pliable personalities who were under the powerful influence of a charismatic leader among the disciples such as Peter. As a result of the stress caused by his denying Jesus and failing to do anything to avert the crucifixion, Peter had, himself, experienced an individual hallucination, perhaps as he desperately sought some form of forgiveness for his failures. These communal hallucinations formed the basis for a series of 'appearance narratives' which, confusingly for people living in the twenty first century, disguised their origin by including individuals with varying psychological dispositions as well as individuals, such as James and Paul, who were not followers of Jesus prior to the crucifixion. Such an explanation for the appearance narratives is *possible*, but I must confess that it requires me to stretch the source material to the limit. I am also left wondering whether such an explanation can adequately account for the remarkably robust faith, not only of Paul, but also of the other disciples.

When looking at a non-physical interpretation of the appearance narratives, I am left, therefore, with the same choices I face when exploring a physical interpretation of them: I must accept that they reflect the resurrection, strange as it may seem, as a real, (though, in this case, spiritual or 'hyper-physical') event, or I must postulate either that a series of genuinely novel hallucinations occurred or that relatively mundane hallucinations occurred that, by chance, were recorded in ways that made them appear to be novel. In truth, this is all very confusing and I must confess that any of these explanations *could* be true. Unless I am either a materialist or a Christian fundamentalist (which I am not), on the basis of my examination so far, I cannot *definitively* rule any explanation out, but that, of course, does not mean that I ought not to press on in the hope that I can come to a conclusion with regard to which offers the most *likely* explanation.

To recap: as far as I can tell there are really only three viable ways of understanding Paul's and the other disciples' experiences: Jesus' resurrection was real and physical, Jesus' resurrection was real and non-physical (whether 'spiritual' or 'hyper-physical'), or belief in the resurrection was the result of a series of individual and communal hallucinations that the disciples failed to understand did not have any basis in objective fact.

Each of the above theories holds some attraction for me. Physical resurrection represents the simplest reading of the source documents and it readily explains the depth and tenacity of the first disciples' faith; it also provides a means of settling very clearly the question of God's existence. Either 'spiritual' or 'hyper-physical' resurrection provides, to my twenty-first century mind, a more accessible understanding of resurrection, removing any need for speculation with regard to the physics of what happens to corpses in the process of resurrection and it encourages me to treat the source documents in a nuanced manner, with historical rigour, as documents of their time. A psychological/hallucination theory removes any requirement for belief in supernatural agency and supports my basic leaning towards scepticism and atheism.

Equally, each of the theories has its problems. Physical resurrection is psychologically difficult to embrace because it requires me to believe that matter was transformed in a manner that defies both my experience and my understanding of physics, chemistry and biology. It also raises questions with regard to the resurrection of other human beings, especially those whose bodies have been completely annihilated; if a transformation of their physical bodies is not necessary for them to be resurrected, it cannot be the case that such a transformation was *necessary* for Jesus. It is, after all, what happens to the *essential person* that matters, not what happens to a corpse. In the case of Jesus, I acknowledge, however, while a transformation of his corpse might not have been necessary, it might still have been *desirable*, perhaps as a sign to his followers.

Non-physical resurrection does not conform to a 'plain reading' of the source documents. In honesty, it also feels as if it is a bit of a compromise between faith and scepticism although it still requires me to embrace the need for direct supernatural intervention; a challenge to my sceptical mind. A psychological/hallucinatory theory is convoluted and tenuous; I imagine a similarly tenuous theory advocating belief in physical resurrection would be given short shrift by most people. It also provides a very shaky foundation for the very vibrant faith of the first disciples. Of course, what I find attractive or problematic does not, in itself, settle anything; it simply helps me to understand better my own reactions to various explanations for the resurrection. It remains clear that *something* gave rise to the appearance narratives and to belief in the resurrection, however unlikely that something might have been.

The appearance narratives are not, of course, the only factors to be taken into account in an investigation of the resurrection. The resurrection narratives also include accounts of the followers of Jesus finding his tomb to be empty on 'the third day' following his crucifixion. The significance of the empty tomb, along with some very physical features attributed to the risen Jesus in the appearance narratives, also requires investigation.

The Empty Tomb and Physical Aspects of the Resurrection Narratives

In looking, *as dispassionately as possible*, at the empty tomb narratives, I believe that three broad areas of interpretation deserve exploration: they can be taken at face value as essentially 'literal' accounts, they can be seen as stylised 'true-but-not-literally-true' accounts or they can be viewed as purely legendary additions to the appearance narratives. The border between the first two options is indistinct, but they both stand in contrast to the third option. Once again there are both positives and negatives associated with each of these explanations.

Treating the empty tomb stories as historical reports in a sense similar to that understood in the twenty first century has the merit of simplicity, favouring a 'straightforward' reading of the source documents. This is almost certainly the way most people, Christian and non-Christian alike, read the Gospel narratives. Nonetheless, there are problems associated with this approach that deserve attention.

There are, undoubtedly, differences in the accounts that ought not readily to be dismissed as matters of unimportant detail. The identity and number of women who went to the tomb varies from account to account with Mark naming three women, Matthew two and Luke giving an indeterminate number of, initially, unnamed women, three of whom he later names (John mentions only Mary Magdalene). Mary Magdalene and 'another Mary' are common to the Synoptic Gospel accounts, but other names vary. Mark and Luke record that the women went to the tomb in order to anoint Jesus' body while Matthew states that they set out simply to visit it (John does not say why Mary Magdalene went to the tomb 'while it was still dark', but records that Jesus' body had been anointed with spices by Nicodemus and Joseph of Arimathea *prior* to its interment). In Mark, the women arrived at the tomb to find that the stone had, unexpectedly, been rolled away from the tomb entrance; *entering it* they were met by a *young man* seated in an otherwise empty tomb. In Matthew, the women were met by a *single angel* who was clothed in a snow-white garment and whose face shone 'like lightning'. This angel had descended from heaven, alarming a guard of soldiers (mentioned only in Matthew) who fainted with fear. The angel then sat on the tomb-stone and delivered a message to the women who stood *outside* the tomb listening. In Luke, the women found that the stone had been rolled away, they *entered* the tomb, but saw nothing until suddenly *two men* dressed in dazzling clothes, 'appeared to them'. Luke also records that Peter later ran to the tomb and found it empty, going away puzzled (John records that Mary returned to the tomb after having first run to tell the disciples that the tomb was empty and only then stooped to look into the tomb where she saw *two angels* seated where Jesus' body had lain).

The message delivered by the young man/men/angel/angels also varies from account to account. In Mark and Matthew, the women were told that Jesus had risen and that they were to go to the disciples and tell them that he would meet them in Galilee. In Luke, the women were told that Jesus had risen, but were not given any message to deliver to the disciples. In the truncated ending of Mark's Gospel the women did not meet with the risen Jesus and they, initially, said nothing to anyone because they were frightened and bewildered. Matthew records that they ran to give the disciples the angel's message because they were filled with joy as well as fear and on their way they met with Jesus who echoed the angel's message, instructing the disciples to go to Galilee where they would meet him. Luke states that the women (still an indeterminate number, though three of them are now named) ran to tell the disciples about their experience at the tomb, but no mention is made of them meeting Jesus (John records that Mary

Magdalene met with Jesus in the garden of the tomb, having first of all mistaken him for a gardener).

Mark (shorter ending) does not record any appearances of Jesus, Matthew very briefly records a single appearance to a number of disciples on a hillside in Galilee, while Luke (and John) record quite detailed appearances of Jesus to the disciples, located in or near Jerusalem (John's post-script records a further appearance of Jesus at the Sea of Galilee).

In addition to the differences between the various Gospel accounts outlined above, Matthew alone recounts the story of a guard of soldiers being placed on the tomb who were subsequently bribed by the Jewish authorities not to speak of their experiences. He also includes an account of the resuscitation/resurrection of 'saints' who had been buried near Jerusalem, appearing to a number of people following Jesus' resurrection. All of the Gospels record that Jesus' body was given to Joseph of Arimathea, by Pilate, for burial and that he (along with Nicodemus in John's Gospel) placed the body of Jesus in a new tomb close to the place of crucifixion; a tomb that according to Matthew, belonged to Joseph.

Various attempts have been made by numerous authors and preachers to harmonise these accounts. It *is* possible to weave a fairly complex narrative that blends together the combined details found in the Gospels, although it requires quite a lot of twisting and turning to get the number and location of the angels to agree and it also requires introducing the hypothesis that Jesus initially appeared to the disciples in Jerusalem rather than Galilee because they refused to listen to the women's account of what had taken place at the tomb. It also involves accepting at face value some, frankly very strange, material found in Matthew: the account of the 'saints' rising from the dead and the narrative surrounding the guard of soldiers at the tomb, as well as the rather spectacular appearance of the angel who rolled away the stone from the tomb entrance.

Such endeavours, however, might not only be unnecessary, but, to an extent, misguided. *If*, as many (though by no means all) scholars believe, the Gospels have much in common with the 'lives' of famous people written at that period in the Graeco-Roman world, it is possible to argue that while the Gospel narratives are based on what their authors believed to be core facts with regard to Jesus, individual narratives could be shaped *with limited editorial freedom* to indicate the *meaning and significance* of Jesus' life. In other words, while the authors of the Gospels concurred with the Pauline formula that Jesus had died, been buried and had risen from the dead, they were free, within limitations, to present 'stylised' accounts of the resurrection in keeping with their particular purposes in writing. This, of course, is not how we think of history or biography being written today (although a degree of 'manipulation' of source material is always, in fact, inevitable). It was, however, how careful and thoughtful authors of 'lives' wrote in the first century Roman Empire. It was *entirely acceptable* to conflate events, to write speeches that were not verbatim accounts *but which were based on a core of 'hard' material* and which echoed what was known of an individual's life or teaching and to present narratives that were expanded, *dramatic* versions of what had actually happened. *If* the Gospels fall into this general category of writing and are viewed from this perspective, the accounts of the empty tomb and subsequent 'appearances' of Jesus *still reflect an actual resurrection*, but the accounts presented in the Gospels represent stylised, 'amalgamated' accounts drawn from various sources. The Gospels are, in some respects, closer to modern docudramas than they are to documentaries. This view does not seek to undermine the 'reliability' of the Gospels in any way, but rather, to recognise the sort of literature that the Gospels represent.

In this understanding of the Gospels, the empty tomb narratives could, therefore, reflect *either* the fact that the tomb was, indeed, empty *or* they could represent a 'dramatic' means of emphasising the reality of the later resurrection encounters. The latter is *not* the same as saying that they were fabricated stories without any basis in fact; the relevant 'fact', being the resurrection of Jesus. While this literary device is foreign to modern historians, the authors of 'lives' utilised it with skill; being careful, however, not to undermine the *essential historicity* of their accounts. Such authors were not free to invent their subjects or the main features of their characters and lives, but they were free to 'illustrate' these features in ways that they thought best illuminated the points they wished to highlight.

Alternatively, the Gospel accounts of the empty tomb might be *purely legendary*: stories *created* to convey belief, but which either have *no basis in fact at all* or which were based on a misunderstanding of actual events. For example, just as the appearance narratives *might* have arisen from the first disciples' hallucinations, the empty tomb narratives *might* have arisen from the tomb being found to be empty by female followers of Jesus, perhaps because Joseph of Arimathea had used his tomb as a temporary resting place for Jesus' body (because of the impending Sabbath) and had taken the first opportunity to bury it formally in a cemetery reserved for criminals, just outside Jerusalem. This does, of course, require me to believe that Joseph either never tried to set the record straight or that his protestations were overlooked in the light of the subsequent resurrection faith of the disciples.

The various 'physical' details given by Luke and John in their appearance narratives, such as Jesus eating food, can be interpreted in much the same way as the empty tomb accounts. It is possible to argue that accounts of Jesus eating, of him being touched by his disciples and of him appearing and disappearing at will are literally true, are 'stylised' accounts or are purely legendary.

Resurrection Faith

When I review what the New Testament has to say about the *event* of the resurrection, I find myself faced with a genuine conundrum. I think that it is certain, beyond reasonable doubt, that the first disciples truly believed that Jesus experienced resurrection: he continued to live, after his crucifixion, in a transformed human state. Equally, I do not believe that it is certain, beyond reasonable doubt, that, *in purely historical terms*, I can identify the *precise* basis for this belief.

I believe that Paul's writings and the Gospel narratives can reasonably be interpreted in a more or less literal manner, indicating that a 'physical' resurrection took place and that this was the basis for the disciples' faith. At the same time, Paul's writings and the Gospels can reasonably be read in a non-literal manner, indicating that a 'spiritual' or 'hyper-physical' resurrection took place and that this formed the basis for the disciples' faith. Finally, it is *possible* that the resurrection *faith* of the disciples was genuine, but ultimately misplaced, being based on purely psychological experiences and bolstered by the creation of legends that came, mistakenly, to be interpreted as historical facts. Unless I come to the subject with a closed mind, asserting either that God definitely does or does not exist, I cannot see that I can say *with absolute certainty* which of the above general theories is right or which of them is definitely wrong. No matter which explanation for the disciples' resurrection faith I advocate, based solely on the evidence of the New Testament documents, I have to do so with a degree of uncertainty. If I fashion my life in the light of my understanding of the resurrection, *whether accepting or rejecting it as reflecting reality*, I must do so as a matter of belief, not indisputable fact.

It might be argued that I ought, therefore, to embrace an agnostic view and admit that, since I cannot be absolutely certain with regard to the nature of the resurrection event, I ought to stand aloof from it. I do not find this approach helpful, however, since absolute certainty is seldom available to me when I make important decisions in my life. I cannot be certain whether or not the job I am applying for will be the right one for me, whether or not the woman I am asking to marry me truly loves me or whether or not the journey I am setting out on will end in a safe arrival at my destination or in a fatal accident. I make important decisions on the basis of what I *consider* to be reasonable grounds for so acting. I cannot see any reason why my interpretation of the resurrection ought to be any different; withdrawn agnosticism is not for me.

My consideration of what constitutes reasonable grounds for interpreting the resurrection, and consequently my attitude to *Christian* belief will include more than my appraisal of the New Testament documents. As I have stated already, I shall also employ my intuition and my experiences of life in coming to an eventual conclusion. Nonetheless, I think that it is incumbent upon me to come to some sort of provisional conclusion solely on the basis of my review of the New Testament.

As I have outlined, each of the general theories providing an explanation for the disciples' belief has its attractions and its problems. I am aware that for most of my life I have been an advocate of physical resurrection and a more or less literal reading of the Gospel narratives, acknowledging the explanatory power that this has for the first disciples' faith and for the expansion of the Christian Church. Without rejecting this or viewing it as being at all *untenable*, I cannot say that this is the *only tenable* reading of the Gospel accounts. The change in my attitude is fuelled by allowing the differences in the narratives to have their full effect on me rather than *setting out* to harmonise them. It is also based on an acknowledgement that the Gospels *might be* akin to the 'lives' of famous individuals current at the time and, as such, were meant to be understood as conveying truth, but not *necessarily* through what might be called 'literal history'.

A spiritual or hyper-physical understanding of the resurrection has a strong appeal for me as it makes sense of the disciples' faith while allowing for the possible stylised nature of the Gospel narratives. It does, however leave the question of the empty tomb ambiguously open (so to speak) and that, I find, frustrating (for example, the accounts *could* be figurative, the body *could* have been moved or the tomb could have been empty because the body of Jesus was 'consumed' by a unique act of God). The thought that the disciples' resurrection faith was based on one or more hallucinations, I struggle to view as being credible, given the absolute centrality of belief in the resurrection of Jesus for the Christian faith from its very inception. Nonetheless, partly because of my innate scepticism, I feel the effects of its gravitational pull on me and, rationally, I cannot rule it out entirely.

I would have to say at this stage of my enquiry, based on the evidence found in the New Testament documents, that I would list in order of overall *appeal* those explanations that suggest a spiritual or hyper-physical resurrection occurred, those that suggest a transformed-physical resurrection took place and, lagging some distance behind these 'neck and neck' options, those that suggest that belief in the resurrection can best be understood in purely psychological terms. I fully appreciate that others might order their list differently and that the *appeal* of a particular theory does not imply its truth. If continued analysis of the source documents by scholars was to indicate that the Gospels lie more towards the 'literal history' end of the spectrum than the Graeco-Roman 'lives' end, I should say that transformed-physical resurrection shades either spiritual or hyper-physical resurrection, regardless of which theory I find more appealing. Either way, my lists reflect the fact that I cannot escape the force of the absolute nature of the first disciples' faith; a faith that I find difficult to comprehend other than by accepting that the disciples had a series of real encounters with a resurrected Jesus.

As is no doubt evident, I am not dogmatic about *the nature* of the resurrection of Jesus; in truth, my view tends to oscillate between physical and non-physical resurrection. Much as my scepticism pulls me towards believing in a psychological explanation for the resurrection faith of the first disciples, I simply cannot allow it to overrule my reasoned enquiry which indicates that the resurrection of Jesus is, in some form, a reality. Once again, I admit that I might be wrong, but I might also be right. At the very least, I think that it is reasonable to argue that there is ample in the New Testament accounts to encourage me to continue to explore the veracity of Christian belief, including belief in the existence of God.

That I am unable to produce a 'knock-down' argument, based on the evidence of the New Testament, with regard to the resurrection of Jesus, is not a disappointment to me. As I have stated previously, the existence of God cannot be something that can be *proved* from reasoned argument; if such were the case, then belief in God would become coercive. If I had been able to produce an overwhelmingly convincing argument that the resurrection occurred, *either* as a physical or non-physical reality, then, in effect, I would have produced a 'proof' for God's existence as I cannot really see how resurrection can be viewed as a 'natural' phenomenon. Instead, I have come to a provisional conclusion in favour of belief in the resurrection of Jesus that I think is reasonable, but not compelling.

Chapter Fifteen

The Game Changers-Intuition and Experience
(Intuition and Making Sense of Reality… the Limits of Experience)

How We Really Make Decisions

I said in the first chapter of this book that when it come to making important decisions, most of us do so by dipping into a 'reservoir' containing '*reason, personal experience, psychological disposition, analytical aptitude, aesthetic appreciation, family background, spirituality and peer influences, all mixed together and seasoned with varying quantities of gut-feeling.*' I then condensed this list to the trinity of reason, intuition and experience, suggesting that each plays a distinctive and crucial part in enabling us not only to decide what we think, but also to become what we are.

In the context of enquiring into *Christian* theology, I suggest that one role that reason plays is to map out defensible areas for further investigation by intuition and experience. For example, I do not believe that it is reasonable to spend time investigating whether or not elves exist; disappointing as it might be to devotees of Middle Earth, reason suggests that there is nothing to indicate that they do. Alternatively, reason indicates that God *might, very well,* exist and that Jesus *might, very well,* have experienced resurrection. The possibilities of God existing and Jesus having experienced resurrection are significant enough to warrant further investigation. This, I believe is as far as reason can take me; the rest is down to intuition and experience.

I suspect that many people will recoil from such a thought; after all, in many circles reason enjoys a unique position of respect, bordering in some cases on adulation. While such might be the case, it does not alter the fact that reason has its limits and that those who argue otherwise do so not on the basis of reason, but, I suspect, on the basis of their own intuition and experience of life. In many areas of life, intuition and experience are the real 'game-changers'. I propose that when it comes to our fundamental beliefs about God and theology, this is very much the case.

I have already argued that *if* God exists, reason cannot *prove* that such is the case, primarily because this would make belief coercive. I have also argued that *if* God exists, God would be accessible to all people, including people with limited powers of reason. I also suggest that *if* God exists and is personal, intuition and experience, which are unique to each individual and which cannot be shared or demonstrated publicly in quite the same way as can reason, are likely to be pivotal in God relating to individuals. Similarly, if God does not exist, our decisions to believe or not to believe are likely to emerge from our personal intuition and experience rather than from a use of pure reason. Intuition and experience really are the game-changers.

Intuition and a Theory of Everything

In the next few paragraphs, I intend to look at a number of areas in which I am aware that my intuition plays an important part in my appreciation of reality. I acknowledge that my natural inclination towards scepticism can also be understood as being intuitive; hence, I shall accept that this forms something of a backcloth to my other reflections. I do not expect to come to any definite conclusions based on the following survey, but I do expect that my reflections will inform whatever conclusions I finally reach.

In spite of my continuing inclination towards scepticism noted above, I find it difficult to escape the thought that the existence of God is, in fact, a most satisfactory 'theory of everything'. Given the fact that the evidence available through scientific enquiry may be interpreted either in a theistic or in an atheistic way this comes as no surprise. If God exists, a variety of conundrums are satisfactorily answered; conundrums that otherwise require very complex solutions. While the simplest explanation is not always the right one, I do have to take seriously the explanatory power of a theistic explanation of everything.

This theory explains not only the existence and order of the universe, but also the sense of awe that I have when observing or contemplating it. It explains the intuitive sense that something as grand as the universe is meaningful and purposeful. As I have stated earlier, such intuitive feelings do not *prove* anything, but neither ought they to be dismissed out of hand. To put it differently: if I had no sense of awe at all when thinking of the universe or if I found the thought that it could have meaning or purpose a ridiculous one, then these reactions might undermine belief in God's existence. The fact that my experience of the universe causes me to respond as I do, suggests that this *might* indicate a fundamental resonance with reality.

I also have an innate sense that I and other human beings are of value and that our lives are significant, I find it impossible to act as if we are just an amalgamation of atoms and molecules that combine in particular patterns for a few years and then disappear forever. What we do to one another, to other creatures and to our environment *matters*. If God exists, it is easy to see how all of these intuitive feelings are well-founded; if God does not exist I struggle to find a satisfactory reason to believe that I am really of any significance at all. Certainly, I can claim that since I exist as a sentient being, I might as well make the most of it and invest my existence with a self-declared significance. To be truthful, however, this comes uncomfortably close to whistling in the dark. I should rather accept that I really am of no great significance and simply put up with the unsavoury thought. If God exists, however, I need have no such struggle.

A similar point may be made with regard to morality. I believe that I am a moral being and that it is important that I and others act in morally correct ways. While I might not always be sure of what the correct moral path is and might engage other people in debate over moral issues, the conviction that I am, and ought to be, a moral being remains strong. If God exists, this innate moral sense is entirely understandable; if God does not exist I am left to perform mental gymnastics in an effort to demonstrate that humans *ought* to act morally. I find arguments that a moral sense is a useful evolutionary tool unpersuasive and I cannot find a convincing rebuttal to the assertion that, if morality is a social convention there is nothing *wrong* in acting in any way I please as long as I am not caught and punished by society for any perceived misdeeds. If God exists, it is easy to see why such things as discrimination, racism and the holocaust are repugnant. If God does not exist, utterly objectionable as it may be, all of these can be dismissed as matters of opinion. Some 'extreme' commentators have suggested that such is, indeed, the case. I am intrigued to find how often, at this point, many 'pure' rationalists resort to essentially irrational arguments to bolster their innate sense of morality. If, however, we use intuition as well as rationality in decision-making, *because that is the way God intends us to be*, an innate sense of morality makes sense.

My appreciation of art, music and nature are all explicable and I am free to rejoice in them if God exists. I cannot help but think that if God does not exist all of these are tinged with a certain sense of sadness and even futility. Wonderful creations such as *Hamlet*, Rachmaninov's *Vespers* and Monet's water lilies, as well as my children's playschool finger paintings, greatly enrich my life and I feel that they are valuable in and of themselves. If, as I have suggested, God is inherently creative, these things are all mirrors of the divine spark within us; if God does not exist, what stops them from being just things?

The presence of religion and spirituality around the globe and down through the millennia are perfectly understandable if God exists. Other explanations, of course, exist, but I have to confess that I do not find them terribly convincing. That does not make them incorrect, but the universal existence of spirituality and religion represent a conundrum that I feel is too easily dismissed by many commentators. Religion and spirituality, of course, fall into place if God exists; they are awkward boulders in the intellectual landscape if God does not.

I recognise, therefore, that very many of my intuitive reflections concur with belief in the existence of God and are underlined by it. I also acknowledge that they struggle to find meaning and explanation if God does not exist. This, of course, does not mean that they are correct, but whether I like it or not, I have to accept that there is much in my intuition to support the idea of the existence of God and little, other than my strong natural tendency towards scepticism, to oppose it. Intuitively, I am drawn to recognize the appeal of theism and the sense that it makes of the universe while, at the same time, intuitively, I am wary of such belief. In short, the tug of war continues, but theism would appear to have more weight pulling on its team than atheism.

Personal Experience

If God exists and is anything like the *theodigm* I have suggested, then it is inevitable that people will believe that they have experienced God for themselves. Such, of course, is the case: quite literally, millions of people down through the centuries have been convinced that God's presence has been central to their lives. While this does not indicate that their beliefs were well-founded, it would be a major problem for *Christian* belief in God's existence if such beliefs were either rare or non-existent.

By and large, however, one person's experience tends to have a very limited effect on other persons' belief and it is easy to see why this is so. By its nature, personal experience is *personal* and cannot easily be communicated, never mind transferred, to others. Even communal experiences tend to be subject to varying interpretations by those involved and are not always easily shared with those outside the original participating group. This makes the first disciples' reported experiences of encounters with the risen Jesus all the more distinctive. Nonetheless, if God exists, personal experience will play an important part in helping to create or to nurture belief.

My own experience indicates that belief in God is credible, although, as I have already outlined, I believe that God acts in such a way as to enable, but not to enforce, belief. As such, personal experience may, indeed, have confirmatory significance for individuals, but will almost certainly carry little weight for others. After much hesitation, I have chosen to illustrate this with a particular example from my own life. I do so, not because I want to publicise my own experience, but because I am able to critique my experience more thoroughly than the experiences of others.

As I mentioned at the beginning of this book, I have been involved with Christian churches and groups for most of my life. I think that I have experienced just about every type of worship and have attended just about every kind of church service available across the Christian spectrum. From the clinical grandeur of Westminster

Abbey and the mystery of Greek Orthodox worship to the measured logic of the ALPHA course and the heated fervour of American revivalism, I have seen most of it. I have experienced 'laying on of hands' and have encountered an array of responses from people receiving 'ministry' ranging from stoic resistance, through cool indifference to, quite literally, people frothing at the mouth. The point of this is to say that, prior to the experience I am about to relate, I was no stranger to the many, varied forms of Christian spirituality and practice. I also need to point out that on those occasions where I experienced 'the laying on of hands', I felt and experienced absolutely nothing even though, at times, others around me were obviously affected by their own experiences. In October 1994, however, that changed.

Along with my wife I attended a Sunday evening service at an Anglican church in Dublin where a friend of mine was the minister. I had heard that his church was experiencing what journalists were later to call 'The Toronto Blessing', a phenomenon where people claimed to have powerful physical and emotional reactions to God's presence. In truth, I attended the service with a mixture of scepticism, interest and caution, particularly wary that I should be asked to participate in something that might cause me embarrassment. The service was typical of the 'charismatic' churches of the time: extended singing of worship songs followed by a talk lasting about half and hour and concluding with a time of 'prayer-ministry'. During this time I watched with interest as a number of people walked forward to be prayed for by my friend and others on the 'ministry team'. As anticipated, some of them fell to the floor or shook, in keeping with the accounts that I had heard from previous services. This, I found interesting, but not particularly unusual as I had seen such phenomena before, on many occasions. After about fifteen minutes of observing others being prayed for I walked to the front of the church and, in a spirit of experimentation, asked my friend to pray with me.

I had noted that the standard procedure was that he placed one of his hands lightly on the head of the person being prayed for. As I stood in front of him with my eyes open, I indulged in a stage-whispered, '… no pushing allowed'. As he raised his right hand he began a prayer which started with the word, 'Father'. Before he had time to say anything else and while his hand was still some distance from my head, I experienced something that is difficult to describe but which is vividly imprinted upon my memory.

I immediately felt myself falling, without either volition or any ability to arrest the fall. I did not collapse or lose consciousness although I experienced an initial intense 'fuzziness' in my head; rather I toppled like a tree being felled, remaining almost perfectly straight. As I fell, I rotated, ending up face down on the carpeted floor. I felt as if I was observing the experience in slow motion; rather like experiences of car crashes that I have been in. On one occasion in the past, I had come close to fainting as a relatively minor, but very painful, wound was rather vigorously cleaned by an over enthusiastic nurse, but this feeling was not at all similar. As I lay on the carpet my body was struck by a series of 'surges' that I can only describe as being like electric shocks without the pain; I have, on a couple of occasions, received nasty electric shocks but their effects were quite different from this. I was aware that every few seconds my back arched and my arms and legs convulsed as I felt a new 'surge'. While I was entirely conscious of these movements and was aware that they must have made me look like a stranded fish, I was completely unable to resist them happening in any way. They continued for about forty five minutes at the end of which time I was able to rise shakily to my feet and stagger away from the front of the church.

My first reaction as I fell, was to think, 'My God, there really is a God' which was followed by the thought, 'Oh no, there really is a God' as I became rather acutely aware of my shortcomings. While on the floor, my mind filled with thoughts of God's empathy for the poor, the oppressed and the marginalized and my and other Christians' failure to feel the same way. I was fully aware of the sounds of prayer and worship going on around me, but I kept my eyes closed in order to concentrate on my thoughts. Every now and then the 'surges' would grow stronger; I was later to find out from my wife that this coincided with members of the church's 'ministry team' standing over me and praying silently without me knowing that they were there.

After I had gathered my body up from the floor I tried to gather my thoughts, declining further invitations to be prayed with. Later that night I drove home; a journey of just over one hundred miles, during which my wife and I discussed my experience. The next morning I felt as if I had run a marathon while suffering from the 'flu. I was unable to get out of bed for two days; it was almost as if my body was recovering from a major trauma.

The aftermath of my unusual experience would take much too long to tell, but it may suffice to say that it was not met with anything like universal approval by most other clergy or by many members of the church in which I was a minister. I could not deny what had happened, but my life would have been much more straightforward had it not occurred. It also put paid to what was, until then, a quite promising ecclesiastical career.

This is not the place to talk about those consequences, but rather to reflect on the experience and to seek to see what, if anything, it might have to contribute to belief in the existence of God and the truth or otherwise of *Christian* theology. This might seem to be a strange thing to say; would such an experience not irrevocably convince me of God's existence and assure me of my faith? Surprising as it might be, the answer is 'no'. The experience was so peculiar, and it had so many unwelcome consequences, that I quickly had to examine every detail of it to see if I could explain it satisfactorily in any way other than seeing it as an experience of God's presence. Frankly, I am uncomfortable in putting it into writing and sharing it with a wide audience. I can imagine that some of my current colleagues and acquaintances, on hearing of this for the first time, will now begin to give me a wide berth. Nonetheless, I cannot but be honest and stand by the experience outlined above.

I fully understand that anyone reading about my experience is likely to dismiss it as some form of psychological 'blip', caused, perhaps, by peer pressure or wishful thinking. If I were to view my experience from the 'outside' I, too, would probably opt for this explanation. I do, however, have the advantage of being able to present an analysis from the 'inside'.

I am absolutely certain that whatever caused my experience, it was neither peer-pressure nor wishful thinking. I had been at many services and conferences over the years where I had seen similar scenes to those I witnessed prior to being prayed with on the night in question. I had also been prayed with on many of these occasions and had experienced nothing out of the ordinary. I was under no pressure 'to perform' or to conform to the expectations of others; if anything, I was known to be unreceptive to such 'ministry'. The person praying with me was a friend whom I had known for more than fifteen years and with whom I had been to college; there was no question of my being caught up in any personality cult. My attitude was one of cautious openness to whatever might happen when I was being prayed with, but I certainly did not go to the front of the church *seeking* any particular experience. If anything, I erred on the side of being resistant to anything that would cause me to act in some of the peculiar ways I had observed in others.

At the same time, my experience was both unexpected and totally involuntary. As I have said, I was fully conscious all the time and was aware of all that was happening to me. I did not experience any 'dissociation' or any altered state of consciousness that I was aware of. I did not see any visions or hear any voices. I did find the thoughts outlined above, running with some persistence through my mind, but other than that, the experience was entirely physical. There is no doubting that the event occurred much as I have described it; my wife and others later described what they saw from their perspectives and it tallied with my own account. The burning question for me is, 'what caused it?'

At one level, it is clear to me that my experience was caused by my brain. The total loss of balance, the sense of energy 'surges' and the uncontrollable movements of my back, arms and legs, all have physiological explanations. Certain forms of brain activity caused my muscles to react in certain ways, also 'enabling' me to experience certain sensations such as 'energy surges' in the manner that I described above. The core question, however, remains; what caused my brain to act in this way?

I have no doubt that it would be possible for scientists to replicate the physical aspects of my experience by stimulating various parts of my brain, perhaps by using finely tuned electrodes. Similarly, I imagine that if I were to be close to a truly catastrophic event the physical effects of shock might cause me to react in ways that, in some respects, might be similar to my experience. To be truthful, I am less certain of this as I have, in fact, been in car crashes, been close to bomb explosions and have been caught up in extreme rioting (as an observer, I hasten to add) and have not experienced any obvious physical effects, but, in theory at least, I accept that shock might cause me to act in a very odd manner. In the case of my experience in church, however, my brain was not subjected to external electrical stimulation or to an external physical shock. Again, I have to ask, 'what caused my experience?'

I can honestly rule out any manipulation on the part of my friend. As I have said, I was not susceptible to any psychological influence from him and I am certain that he did not have some hidden electrical device with which he shocked me. The experience was painless, his hand did not come into contact with my head and the church was a taser-free zone.

I have no doubt, however, that *something* external to me caused my experience. I have been prayed with on many subsequent occasions and I have not had a comparable experience, even when, in truth, I rather hoped that I would. I cannot think of anything that was going on in my mind that could have caused my experience and while this does not mean that there could not have been some hidden psychological cause behind my experience, I have to acknowledge that neither at the time, not since, have I been able to come close to identifying what it might have been.

My experience certainly felt as if I was 'hit' by some form of energy, but what that was, I cannot identify with certainty. If its source was my friend, it is odd that even though he prayed with me on many subsequent occasions, I never felt anything similar. My experience happened in the context of prayer and it had the effect of causing me to feel as if I had an insight into God's attitude toward the poor and the oppressed. This enables me to consider seriously that my experience was caused by God. The fact that it was not repeated is in keeping with the *theodigm* which suggests that God's actions and existence are not 'provable'. If it was God, then God certainly got my attention, with the experience causing me to take much more seriously such things as compassion, justice and integrity.

The experience, however, did not and does not *prove* God's existence to me. In fact, I discovered that its influence tended to ebb and flow with the fluctuating nature of my spirituality. At times when I prayed and paid attention to the spiritual side of my life, it was influential; at other times, it was little more than a memory. Again, I cannot help but contrast this with the first disciples' adherence to their faith; their 'post-resurrection' experiences must have been stronger and more instructive than mine, remarkable, to me, as it was.

This, I suggest is precisely how experience ought to contribute to belief in God's existence, if God does, in fact, exist. If God exists and is personal, then any experience that I might have of God is going to be personally based. The degree to which that experience is relevant to my life is likely to be strongly affected by the nature of my ongoing relationship with whomever or whatever I perceive God to be.

Without pressing the analogy too far, it may usefully be compared to marriage. I know that I am married to my wife and I am able both to remember the experience of the wedding ceremony and also to appeal to witnesses who observed me taking my marriage vows. Getting married was a genuinely significant experience and I am glad that my wife and I decided to formalise our relationship in that way. The vows that I took and the memory of the wedding have been important to me and for my ongoing relationship with my wife, especially at times when I have had to face difficulties in life. At the same time, I also acknowledge that my memories and the significance of my wedding are strongest when I am attentive to my relationship with my wife and vice versa. We certainly could not live off that one experience and its memory. Continued relationship building, mending and improvement are necessary to give the wedding experience any sense of current 'life'. It is, therefore, not surprising that my various spiritual experiences, while having the capacity to affect and influence my belief in God, do not have the power to copper-fasten it.

Of course, I have also had many experiences in life that indicate to me that, if God exists, God is not the kind of being who acts in the kind of ways, popularly believed by many people. My experience, as well as my theology, indicates that God, *should God exist*, does not intervene in my life in 'directive' ways very often. Similarly, as I have already suggested, God is not some sort of supernatural answer-machine and God does not 'micro-manage' details of human existence. God's nature, and my consequent relationship with what I perceive to be God, are such that God is most interested in the formation of me as a moral, creative being, living as part of a community of moral, creative beings. My experiences, like my intuition, are, therefore instructive, but not, in themselves, definitive.

Postscript

Bridge Painting

In this book, I set out to *investigate* the possibility of God's existence and the subsequent cogency of *Christian* theology: to try to discover whether or not it might be reasonable, coherent and believable. As I draw towards the end of my enquiry, I now seek to come to some conclusions which I shall offer for consideration. I shall do so, not in an attempt to convince, but, rather in a spirit of honesty and transparency. If they assist others as they think their own way through the fascinating topic of God's existence and the insights that might be gained from *Christian* theology, so much the better, but if they don't, the exercise has still been a valuable one for me.

I have tried to be both honest and realistic about my inbuilt prejudices and my ability to counter them. As I have investigated *Christian* theology, I can honestly say that I have genuinely rethought my way through a number of issues and the appreciation of reality that I now have is significantly different, at a number of points, from the understanding I had as I began this journey.

I think that I have a greater appreciation of the roles that intuition and experience *ought* to play both in understanding the nature of reality and in relating to it. This is so, both in principle and in practice. In spite of my continued inbuilt scepticism and natural tendency to elevate a rationalist/scientific approach to life beyond a level where it can, paradoxically, be rationally or scientifically defended, I recognise that life ought to be viewed much more holistically than I was wont to do. This, I have come to respect, is as much true of theological enquiry as it is of any other aspect of life.

My investigation of *Christian* theology has convinced me that it is *compatible* with a defensible understanding of reality, and particularly, with a defensible understanding of the nature of the universe. On the issue of whether matter has arisen from mind or mind from matter, I have professed that I find the former somewhat easier to conceptualize than the latter, but that the reality of this is far from being provable. I am also convinced that *Christian* theology, as I have outlined it, is intellectually robust and coherent, providing a 'theory of everything' that is satisfying and attractive. I have come to the opinion that, based purely on the evidence of the New Testament, it is not possible to prove whether a 'physical', a 'non-physical' or a 'psychological' explanation of the resurrection of Jesus is correct, but I have also suggested that either a non-physical or a physical understanding of the resurrection better explains the existence of the first disciples faith and the growth of the Christian Church, than does a psychological one. This causes me to have a bias in favour of belief in the existence of God, but again, all such reflections fall short of proof.

My reflections on my own intuition and my own varied experiences of life, spiritual and otherwise, indicate that belief in the existence of God is both reasonable and holistically satisfying, but, yet again, this does not prove that God does, in fact, exist or that *Christian* theology is correct. At the same time, they also contribute positively towards my continuing to favour belief.

My conclusions at the end of this study are, therefore, that while neither theism nor atheism is susceptible to proof, this does not mean that I am forever locked into agnosticism. There is enough in *Christian* theology for me to *favour* it as a viable interpretation of reality and to continue *actively* to pursue it through further intellectual exploration, intuitive reflection and, above all, personal experience. I suspect that it will be the constant pursuit of the latter that will really make the difference.

In so doing, I recognise that I can ever only understand and appreciate God through a series of theodigms that I find both defensible and appropriate at any given stage in my life. I do, of course, hope that these theodigms genuinely approximate to the truth and that they will, in fact, lead me to experience something of God.

While, in theory, I might think of God as a 'Supreme being' or as 'Fundamental Mind', in practice, such theodigms, while rationally satisfying, are intuitively, emotionally and psychologically deficient. To the intellectual rigour of 'Fundamental Mind', I need to add something more obviously 'personal'. For this reason, my current theodigm of God not only contains the idea of 'Fundamental Mind', but it also understands God as 'love', which found its full, complex human expression in the person of Jesus of Nazareth. My theodigm also includes a growing appreciation that creativity lies at the very heart of God. Consequently, I believe that love and creativity ought to lie at the heart of humanity. My continued 'pursuit' of God, therefore, will be fashioned not by intellectual inquiry alone, but, in relationship with others I intend to participate in worship, in social action and in personal prayer as well as to develop my appreciation of the arts and of the natural world. Life is full of emotion and experimentation as well as full of reason and reflection; I fully intend to explore all available approaches as I continue my God enquiry beyond the pages of this book. This particular God Enquiry might be drawing to a close, but the God Experiment continues.

So, at the end of my enquiry, I remain by temperament and inclination an atheist, but by persuasion a *Christian*. I do not claim that I have exhausted all possible philosophical enquiries or explored all possible theological avenues (I am aware that further reflection on *mystical theism* beckons), but I am satisfied that I have covered much useful ground. I also suspect that after catching breath and pausing for a while, I shall start painting the bridge all over again…

Supreme creativity   p 91-92

Moral beings, moral choice and existence/belief in God
meaning of incarnation P. 125 ......   ⌐ P 110-115

Death as a limitation of suffering or the ability
to inflict suffering P 136